VOLUME 1

THE IMPACTS OF CENSORSHIP

VOLUME 1

THE IMPACTS OF CENSORSHIP

RESEARCH ON THE INTERSECTION OF CENSORSHIP AND TEACHING ENGLISH

EDITORS
Ann D. David, University of the Incarnate Word
Katharine Covino, Fitchburg State University
Christina L. Dobbs, Boston University
Christine Emeran, National Coalition Against Censorship
Mark Letcher, Lewis University

Copy Editor: Michael Ryan
Staff Editor: Cynthia Gomez
Cover Design: Pat Mayer
Interior Design: Ash Goodwin

ISBN 978-0-8141-0248-0
eISBN 978-0-8141-0249-7
PDF ISBN 978-0-8141-0250-3

It is the policy of NCTE in its journals and other publications to provide a forum for the open discussion of ideas concerning the content and the teaching of English and the language arts. Publicity accorded to any particular point of view does not imply endorsement by the Executive Committee, the Board of Directors, or the membership at large, except in announcements of policy, where such endorsement is clearly specified.

NCTE provides equal employment opportunity to all staff members and applicants for employment without regard to race, color, religion, sex, national origin, age, physical, mental or perceived handicap/disability, sexual orientation including gender identity or expression, ancestry, genetic information, marital status, military status, unfavorable discharge from military service, pregnancy, citizenship status, personal appearance, matriculation or political affiliation, or any other protected status under applicable federal, state, and local laws.

Every effort has been made to provide current URLs and email addresses, but, because of the rapidly changing nature of the web, some sites and addresses may no longer be accessible.

Library of Congress Control Number: 2025932561

VOLUME 1 | THE IMPACTS OF CENSORSHIP

CONTENTS

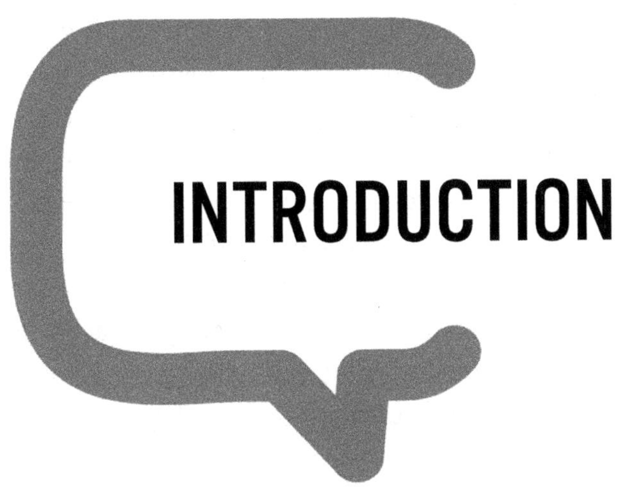

INTRODUCTION

In the wake of the tumultuous events of 2020, the landscape of education in the United States has undergone a seismic shift, marked by an alarming rise in book challenges and bans. This surge, documented by organizations such as the National Coalition Against Censorship, PEN America, and the American Library Association (ALA), reflects a broader political climate that sees classrooms and libraries as fodder for political gain. Once viewed as bastions of intellectual freedom, schools are now sites of contentious debates over curriculum and content, often driven by partisan agendas and conservative advocacy groups masquerading as grassroots movements.

The increase in censorship, particularly regarding books that explore themes of race, gender, sexuality, and violence, has reached crisis proportions. PEN America (Meehan et al., 2024) reported a staggering 10,046 instances of book bans in public schools during the 2023–2024 school year—an increase of over 200 percent from the previous year. This alarming trend highlights a coordinated effort to suppress diverse ideas and narratives that are essential for fostering critical thinking and empathy in students. Similarly, the ALA (2024) documented 4,240 unique book titles challenged in 2023, representing a 65 percent increase from 2022. The majority of these challenges targeted books for teens, particularly those authored by or about BIPOC and LGBTQIA+ individuals (PEN, 2024). This targeting of diverse books reflects a fundamental erosion of educational access. Every bit as damaging, these emerging patterns undermine the ability of students to engage with a wide spectrum of perspectives. Further, these restrictions prevent teachers from accessing the full range of books they need in order to teach the students in their classrooms. Assaulted by censorship in all its forms leaves many English teachers working in a climate of fear. The chilling effect on educators, who worry about the very real repercussions for including diverse voices in their curricula, is palpable and threatens to create a homogenous educational environment devoid of critical inquiry. Battered by such headwinds, teachers feel pushed to self-censor, removing diverse books from classroom shelves and not integrating them into their curriculum (Ginsberg & Chae, this volume).

At the core of this censorship crisis are two interconnected trends: First, the rise of content-restrictive legislation that ostensibly aims to empower parental rights but effectively stifles discussions on critical topics. While Florida and Texas laws were most widely covered in the national media, smaller states like Kentucky, Idaho, and Utah also passed legislation targeting "divisive concepts." These laws seek to limit how educators address issues of race and identity. Since January 2021, 42 states have introduced legislation that restricts the teaching of critical race theory or related subjects, with 17 states enacting such measures by the fall of 2022 (Schwartz, 2024). Two works in this volume discuss the impact of these kinds of laws. Cridland-Hughes et al. (2024) look at the policy environment of South Carolina, and Muir and O'Keeffe (2024) explore how teachers navigated Texas's restrictions on the 1619 Project. By limiting access to texts, this kind of legislation curtails students' intellectual freedom and their ability to develop as critical thinkers able to engage with diverse perspectives. Every bit as troubling are the ways this legislation has politicized school curriculum and book selections far beyond what has happened in the past.

Restrictive legislation has created a real climate of fear for educators. But slowly, in some places, such laws are being challenged. In Florida, Penguin Random House filed suit on behalf of students, teachers, and authors because restricting curriculum materials like books, which HB1069 requires, is government censorship of students' First Amendment rights (PRH, 2023). While the case is still unfolding, the finding that the students had standing represents a win in and of itself. Simply put, the court agreed that students had experienced injury. Texas House Bill 900 (2023) sought to restrict books by ordering booksellers to label books as "sexually explicit." In response, two independent bookstores sued the state based on the infringement of their First Amendment rights. They claimed the state could not order an independent business to "say" anything about a book. The suit won in federal district court and on appeal with the 5th Circuit, which is typically considered a conservative court (Book People, Inc. v. Wong, 2024). Lastly, NCTE and others have signed amicus briefs regarding litigation in Georgia and California. A Georgia teacher is arguing that her firing for reading *My Shadow Is Purple* by Scott Stuart violated Title IX, which protects individuals from discrimination based on sex. The California lawsuit is focused on a school board that restricted books featuring LGBTQ+ characters and telling complex histories of African Americans in the US. These restrictions violate *Board of Education v. Pico* (1982), a Supreme Court ruling that found school boards could not ban curriculum materials simply because they disagreed with them. Litigation takes time, and even a win in court does not mean an immediate end to the climate of fear these laws and challenges created. But litigation reminds everyone—students, teachers, administrators, parents, and community members—that the rule of law does still matter and that the processes established to consider the curriculum in schools can be trusted. These wins carry with them the possibility of hope.

Second, the organized campaigns for mass book bans highlight a strategic shift in how challenges are initiated and pursued. Once the purview of concerned parents, these efforts now draw on broader community coalitions, often fueled by coordinated initiatives from conservative political action groups (Pappano, 2024). Organizations No Left Turn or US Parents Involved in Education have garnered attention for their aggressive campaigns aimed at removing books deemed inappropriate. Such groups take as their special targets literature that addresses LGBTQ issues, racial diversity, and other sensitive subjects. This mobilization is not only about individual titles; it seeks to create comprehensive lists of "objectionable" works that align with a specific conservative ideological agenda. These lists are then shared widely via social media and picked up by individuals or smaller community groups, which then file challenges at their local level (Natanson, 2022). So, while these challenges appear local, the reality is that they are part of a national network that is loosely affiliated but whose hubs are both politically aligned and politically funded (Swenson, 2023). These groups have also inspired more local groups to form and echo their ideology centered on eliminating books from classrooms and libraries (Halpern, 2023).

In light of these organized attempts to restrict books, many different organizations have deepened their work on behalf of the right to read, and engaged citizens have built new organizations. Unite Against Book Bans, founded by the American Library Association, is one such group. Standing strong with over 100 national and local partners across the country, the group seeks to support books, teachers, and librarians by providing resources to anyone looking for ways to stand up to censorship. Looking at statewide organizations, the Texas Freedom to Read Project brings together Texans to support schools and libraries and broadly publicizes incidents of censorship. Similarly, the Florida Freedom to Read Project is a parent-led group that seeks to support public schools and teachers in navigating extremely restrictive curriculum laws through advocacy, information sharing, and building allyship. Even as California teachers and schools are not working under restrictive legislation, Golden State Readers works to draw attention to book bans and other forms of censorship through outreach and advocacy. There is work going on everywhere to support students' right to read and teachers' right to teach.

In this contentious landscape, the imperative to uphold students' rights to read and to explore a rich tapestry of ideas is more crucial than ever. As book bans escalate, the conversation surrounding freedom of expression in public schools must remain at the forefront. Educational institutions should not only be spaces for learning but also incubators of open dialogue and exploration. The stakes are high; the future of our democracy relies on an informed citizenry, capable of understanding and engaging with the complexities of our shared human experience.

NCTE's Role in Fighting Censorship and Protecting Intellectual Freedom

Since the 1950s, NCTE has taken a strong stance against censorship in the classroom. In 1953, spurred by McCarthyism, NCTE published a pamphlet titled *Censorship and Controversy* that held teachers' professionalism and decision making in book selection and curricular design central to "the educational process in a free society" (1953, p. 5). The pamphlet represented the first step in a long lineage of advocacy for intellectual freedom and made clear the organization's belief that "to suppress freedom of thought and inquiry would be both unnecessary and disastrous" (p. 9). Additionally, the booklet centered teachers as educational experts who were in the best position to select books for students without external forces interfering.

> Teachers and school authorities are aware of their responsibilities . . . both to their students and to the people of their communities. Their professional training and their loyalty to American ideals cause them to exert every effort to carry

> on class work in controversial fields in ways that are in accord with American ideals . . . (p. 9)

The foundational elements laid out in this document are still clearly visible in the intellectual freedom work that has continued in the decades since.

Less than a decade after the pamphlet was created, NCTE published the first *Students' Right to Read* (1962) statement. Its language is startlingly prescient:

> Not as sensational, but perhaps more important, are the long-range results [of censorship]. Merely from fear of such attacks, schools have removed enduring books from libraries and classrooms. Many students continue their "education" in a climate hostile to free inquiry, with limited access to important literary documents. (p. 5)

While moving through multiple revisions across the decades, this statement—and the spirit of its words—anchors NCTE's commitment to student access to diverse books and the centrality of teachers' professional knowledge to make informed decisions about selecting books for instructional purposes. At its core, NCTE believes that teachers "possess judgment and understanding and can be trusted with the determination of their own actions" (*Students' Right to Read,* 2018).

NCTE's constituent groups—the Assembly on Literature for Adolescents of NCTE (ALAN), the Conference on English Leadership (CEL), and the Conference on College Composition and Communication (CCCC)—have also taken up the work of intellectual freedom. ALAN's focus on adolescent literature offers multiple opportunities for members to discuss book challenges and censorship, often with some of the very authors whose books are being challenged. The annual ALAN workshop often includes discussions of censorship, and ALAN has maintained a censorship committee to look at challenges to adolescent literature titles across the country. CEL's major constituency consists of English department chairs, leaders, and literacy supervisors, often at the secondary level. Recent CEL conferences have dealt with topics of curriculum development, leading antiracist community building in ELA departments, and preparing teachers to address new laws and challenges to book selections in their respective contexts. CCCC first passed *Students' Right to Their Own Language* in 1972 and reaffirmed it as recently as 2014. This statement centers both students' right to their own dialects as well as the need for teachers to have the experience and training to uphold this right. These groups echo and reinforce NCTE's vocal stances and action-based advocacy against censorship.

National rhetoric, state legislation, and social media have emboldened parents, community members, and even school board officials to insult and attack English teachers and librarians. News media have reported these incidents occurring during school board meetings, on social media, and in the communities. The cumulative impact, and the exponentially growing volume of book challenges and bans, have created a climate of fear for those who select books for children and young people to read. School districts have been overwhelmed by requests to reconsider thousands of book titles. Principals, without clear guidance on how to respond to calls for banning books, have pulled books from classrooms and libraries, book-buying budgets have been slashed, and classroom libraries have been kept in boxes for fear of running afoul of restrictive laws and policies. The risks and costs, financial and personal, to individual English teachers are significant. And as English teachers choose to self-censor out of a desire for self-preservation, or choose to leave the profession entirely, their students and communities suffer that cost.

The Intellectual Freedom Center and the Committee on Censorship

While NCTE has always offered resources to members experiencing censorship, as the contemporary reports of censorship have increased, the need for one-on-one support by an NCTE staff member has also increased. NCTE has long coordinated among its partners—like PEN America, NCAC, and the ACLU—in writing letters to school boards, writing amicus briefs in ongoing litigation around restrictive policies, and weighing in on media accounts of censorship and legislation. The need for these letters has dramatically increased since 2021. NCTE has been a presence on Capitol Hill as Representative Jamie Raskin (D-MD) and Senator Brian Schatz (D-HI) sponsored a resolution to recognize Banned Books Week and to denounce attacks on books and book censorship.

While the news media has often focused on conservative state legislatures enacting laws that serve as educational gag orders (PEN, 2021), the reality of censorship reports to NCTE is that censorship happens in every state and every kind of community. Attendees to convention sessions focused on censorship share stories from urban schools, rural communities, and suburban schools. They note the same types of intellectual freedom challenges whether their state politics are majority Republican or Democratic. With each successive year and the ever-growing number of book challenges, bans, and restrictive legislation, NCTE seeks new ways to support teachers in keeping diverse books in students' hands.

Since 2020, the Intellectual Freedom Center and the Committee Against Censorship have worked together on multiple initiatives that directly support classroom teachers. Central to this work is the This Story Matters Book Rationale Database, launched in 2021. This project involved both digitizing and categorizing legacy book rationales and populating the database with rationales for current releases, texts that members reported as challenged, and books on ALA's Most Challenged list. CAC members worked with NCTE staff to craft a new rationale template and review rubric and then to write rationales. The success of the database was such that the This Story Matters Teacher Corps project was launched, recruiting classroom teachers, ELA administrators, graduate students, and faculty members to write even more rationales. As of the fall of 2024, the database includes more than 1,400 rationales.

In addition to the Book Rationale Database, the CAC sought to keep NCTE members informed of the state of censorship, to validate teachers' experiences of censorship, and to serve as a resource to members. Through virtual and in-person workshops and conference sessions, CAC members crafted opportunities for NCTE members to share their own stories, as well as to engage with the larger contexts for this surge in censorship. Beginning in 2021, the CAC used its sponsored sessions at the NCTE Annual Convention to highlight the emerging data on censorship from the National Coalition Against Censorship, to lift up the voices of those engaging directly in intellectual freedom efforts, and to validate the experiences of classroom teachers experiencing censorship. Teacher-librarian Julia Torres (2021) and author Mindy McGinnis (2023) shared their own experiences with censorship from their different perspectives. Beginning in 2022, NCTE's Banned Books Week webinars featured state affiliates sharing their advocacy for teachers as professionals best positioned to make curricular decisions about books. In the summer of 2022, NCTE hosted its first in-person gathering since 2019, Homecoming in Louisville, Kentucky, and featured CAC members and partners like PEN America and Stand for Children sharing insights on the political and social contexts for censorship and actions teachers could take in their classrooms.

Throughout 2021 and 2022, participants in all of these sessions were moving between disbelief, outrage, and defeat. The stories shared were often painful—teachers being accused of corrupting children for their book selections and then feeling shame that they must have done something wrong; other teachers feeling little to no support from the school's administration when challenges were issued. By 2023, though, the mood had shifted. In the Banned Books Week webinar, the Maine Council for English Language Arts shared their success in stopping restrictive legislation popular in other states before it even left committee. Teachers sharing their stories in the chat were focused on organizing, finding ways to keep books in their classrooms, and feeling confident in their own professionalism. While the 2023 Convention was certainly full of teachers sharing continued stories of censorship in their classrooms and communities, they were also focused on building a network of allies, pushing back against administrators not following curriculum review policies, and centering the importance of students' reading diverse stories. The hope of CAC was that teachers could take ideas back to their school sites, focus on the work and obstacles ahead, and use their network to determine new ways to organize and push back against challenges.

Additionally, the CAC recognized the need to capture this moment through the expertise of scholars. In 2022, the CAC proposed the creation of the Intellectual Freedom Fellowship, a committee-led effort specially funded by NCTE. This fellowship sought to fund emerging research on censorship as it was impacting classroom English teachers. Over 30 applicants applied for the fellowship, and this volume represents some of that scholarly work. Ricki Ginsberg and Kyungae Chae were selected as the fellows, and their national survey of ELA teachers and the impacts of censorship on their book selection is featured as our first chapter. The next three chapters were drawn from applicants for the fellowship who also presented at the NCTE Annual Convention in 2023.

Chapter Summaries

Ginsberg and Chae focus on soft censorship through an examination of the voices of secondary English language arts teachers. Drawing on an overarching, nationwide survey of US teachers' experiences, the study employs mixed methods to better understand how various forms of censorship, and particularly soft censorship, have reduced teacher autonomy and professional treatment, as well as how it has negatively impacted students' critical thinking skills. The findings focus on soft, or quiet, censorship, which is present both discursively and systematically within schools. First, soft censorship occurs through the bureaucratic process of schools including preapproved book lists, various forms of required permissions for using books in instruction, or restrictions on purchasing. Second, individuals with power and access to the books themselves or the processes around selection enact soft censorship in often hidden ways. Finally, teachers engage in quiet censorship through text avoidance—

simply choosing not to use some books for fear of what might happen. When these are taken together, soft censorship impinges upon teachers' ability to teach, and it is devastating to young people's freedom to read. The authors contend that understanding specific instances of censorship, when combined with larger emergent patterns in their data, has the potential to offer tangible solutions for addressing what teachers describe as a highly political, fear-inducing reality that has the potential to drive them out of the classroom.

In "Middle School Teachers' Perceived Autonomy Over Curricular Materials in a Charged Sociopolitical Climate," authors Paciga and Koss investigate middle school teachers' thoughts and reflections regarding their autonomy—defined as capacity, self-direction, and freedom—to select children's literature for their classroom instruction and inclusion in their classroom libraries. Employing qualitative analysis of interview responses of 22 grades 6–8 teachers, the authors analyzed the data set across the three constructs they use to define teacher autonomy. Findings show teachers feel well equipped to select quality literature due to their own identities as avid readers, their networks and expertise at identifying new readings for the classroom, and their desire to be treated as professionals who know their students. Additionally, they are impacted by internal and external factors, including their personal beliefs and district and national restrictions. Overall, though, they report that recent sociopolitical events have stifled their feelings of freedom to make book selections.

In "Challenging Times: Book Challenges and State Consolidation of Power in South Carolina," Cridland-Hughes and her coauthors trace recent legislative and educational policy decisions enacted in South Carolina. Their chief interest in this work is to describe both the process of challenging books and the nature of young adult book challenges, paying particular attention to the types of books challenged and how those align with texts accused of being vehicles of CRT, which is a key component of this recent surge of censorship. The research questions of the study explore these central issues: What is the context of the book challenge as a nested process? How does this intersect with attacks against schools related to critical race theory? Grounding the study within a critical paradigm, the authors approached data analysis through the lens of critical policy analysis (Apple, 2019), which views policies, defined broadly, as artifacts of society, where "the politics and compromises that go into the creation of a policy, and the preferred meanings that are contained within it, need to be critically examined" along with "how the policy is distributed and given authority and power" and how that policy is "received, reinterpreted and even resisted" (Apple, 2019, pp. 280–281). Findings from the study reveal a profoundly undemocratic process at work, which has prompted restrictions, confusion, and concern among South Carolina school districts. During this time of attacks against K–12 schools, this study helps to illuminate where policy power rests and who controls the policies that control curricular freedom.

Muir and O'Keeffe position their piece, "The Meaning of 'Informed American Patriotism': Teaching the 1619 Project in Texas," as a response to Texas Senate Bill 3, legislation aimed at restricting the teaching of critical race theory, as well as promoting patriotism in public school classrooms. Working within the qualitative paradigm, the authors crafted survey questions and shared them with K–12 school-based administrators, ELAR teachers, and librarians to document the immediate effects of the laws on teachers and local school districts. In their responses, educators and administrators identified "workaround" methods of introducing their students to challenged and banned materials like the 1619 Project (The 1619 Project, 2021). The authors' findings highlight the importance of intentional community building, and they forefront instances in which educators learned from each other how to navigate the new laws without compromising course content by building supportive systems for navigating censorship challenges. Results indicate that Texas teachers can preserve some academic freedom through partnerships with institutions of higher learning, such as the local community college and educational nonprofit organizations like the Pulitzer Center Afterschool Partnership. The piece makes clear that Texas teachers who wish to offer their students any opportunities to engage with the 1619 Project should collaborate and partner with allies in the local community.

The final chapter is a reprint of "'Lots of Ways to Be Brave': A Teacher's Guide to Facing Censorship." This article, written by members of NCTE's Committee Against Censorship, offers teachers strategies for preparing for a potential challenge, responding and reporting during a challenge process, and reflecting and repairing after a book challenge. This action-oriented article can serve as an important touchstone for an individual teacher or a discussion piece for a department and includes ideas worth sharing with an administrator.

Conclusion

The research in this volume, as well as additional emerging research about censorship and English teaching, offers some noteworthy findings. First, teachers have the academic training and professional experience to make the best curricular decisions for their students, but ideologically driven parents and community members are overriding that training and experience, inserting themselves into curricular decision making. What teachers need in this charged moment is explicit allyship as a way to rebuild public trust. Second, reading has value, and many people believe in that value. All students have the right to encounter stories that reflect their lives and experiences, as well as the lives and experiences of others. English teachers have the power and potential to use literature as a tool to awaken and instill curiosity, care, critical thinking, empowerment, and hope. That does not mean there will not be moments of discomfort and struggle. Grappling with the darker pieces of our shared history is difficult and instructive in equal parts. But we must embrace and not avoid the challenge this reckoning demands.

The research presented in this volume grows out of this moment and recognizes the importance of marking this moment through empirical research. This work also invites all ELA professionals to consider their role in the work of intellectual freedom and in protecting students' right to read.

References

The 1619 Project. (2019). *The New York Times Magazine.* https://www.nytimes.com/interactive/2019/08/14/magazine/1619-america-slavery.html

American Library Association. (2024, March 14). *American Library Association reports record number of unique book titles challenged in 2023.* https://www.ala.org/news/2024/03/american-library-association-reports-record-number-unique-book-titles#:~:text=CHICAGO%20%E2%80%94%20The%20number%20of%20titles,those%20targeted%20in%20censorship%20attempts

Apple, M. (2019). On doing critical policy analysis. *Educational Policy, 33*(1), 276–287. https://doi.org/10.1177/0895904818807307

Board of Education v. Pico, 457 U.S. 853 (1982). https://www.loc.gov/item/usrep457853

Book People, Inc. v. Wong, 23-50668 F.4th (5th Cir. 2024). https://storage.courtlistener.com/recap/gov.uscourts.ca5.215797/gov.uscourts.ca5.215797.186.1.pdf

Friedman, J., & Tager, J. (2021, November 8). *Educational gag orders*. PEN America. https://pen.org/report/educational-gag-orders/

Halpern, S. (2023, May 18). The fight for the soul of a school board. *The New Yorker*. https://www.newyorker.com/news/dispatch/the-fight-for-the-soul-of-a-school-board

Meehan, K., Baêta, S., Magnusson, T., & Markham, M. (2024, November 1). *Banned in the USA: Beyond the shelves*. PEN America. https://pen.org/report/beyond-the-shelves/

Natanson, H. (2022, December 22). A mom wrongly said the book showed pedophilia. School libraries banned it. *The Washington Post*.www.washingtonpost.com/education/2022/12/22/lawn-boy-book-ban-pedophilia/

National Council of Teachers of English. (1953). *Censorship and controversy*. https://archives.library.illinois.edu/ncte/exhibits/the-fight-against-censorship/

National Council of Teachers of English. (1962). *The students' right to read*. https://archives.library.illinois.edu/ncte/exhibits/the-fight-against-censorship/

Penguin Random House. (2024, August 31). *Penguin Random House, 5 additional publishers, & Authors Guild file landmark lawsuit against state of Florida for unconstitutional book-banning provisions with House Bill 1069.* https://global.penguinrandomhouse.com/announcements/penguin-random-house-5-additional-publishers-authors-guild-file-landmark-lawsuit-against-state-of-florida-for-unconstitutional-book-banning-provisions-with-house-bill-1069/

READER Act, H.R. 900, 88th Leg. (Tex. 2023). https://capitol.texas.gov/tlodocs/88R/billtext/html/HB00900I.htm

Schwartz, S. (2024, November 1). Map: Where critical race theory is under attack. *Education Week*. https://www.edweek.org/policy-politics/map-where-critical-race-theory-is-under-attack/2021/06

Swenson, A. (2023, June 11). *Moms for Liberty rises as power player in GOP politics after attacking schools over gender, race.* Associated Press. https://apnews.com/article/moms-for-liberty-2024-election-republican-candidates-f46500e0e17761a7e6a3c02b61a3d229

National Teacher Report of Quiet and Soft Censorship in United States Public Schools

RICKI GINSBERG
KYUNGAE CHAE

Much of the national rhetoric about book bannings has centered on the thoughts of politicians, parents, and anti-government extremist groups, like Moms for Liberty (Dellinger, 2021; Lopez, 2021; Natanson, 2023), but those who work daily with the students—the teachers—are broadly missing from those conversations. Scholars have studied individual educators' experiences with and attempts to resist censorship (Bachmann & Tellez, 2023; Mitchell, 2023; Smith & Banack, 2024), but these have not netted the same traction as overt forms of censorship in the public. Rather, the current book-banning crusade fueled by partisanism is an attempt to maintain power for those who most often work outside of education, which is an affront to the professionalism and expertise of teachers and a threat to literacy and democracy. Teachers have become subject to reduced autonomy in addressing the interests and needs of their students and are, in some cases, explicitly blocked from providing texts that serve as windows, mirrors, and sliding glass doors for students (Bishop, 2012). This assault on education is a war on critical thinking and literacy and creates an increasingly hostile environment for teachers.

Nonprofit organizations like PEN America, the National Council of Teachers of English, the National Coalition Against Censorship, the American Library Association, and We Need Diverse Books have acted against censorship with supportive teacher resources and censorship indexes. This study complements these organizations' efforts by offering an overarching, nationwide analysis of US teachers' experiences with soft censorship, defined in more detail below. Although smaller studies have offered more general examples of teacher perceptions of censorship (Koss & Paciga, 2023; Nam, 2023; Smith et al., 2018), we sought to understand the quieter forms of censorship along with teachers' experiences nationally. Understanding teachers' experiences related to soft censorship has the potential to offer tangible solutions for addressing what teachers describe as a highly political, fear-inducing reality that has the potential to drive them out of the classroom. The findings reveal that soft censorship appears both discursively and systematically within schools, which impinges upon teachers' ability to teach responsively, but ultimately, it is devastating young people's freedom to read.

The American Library Association describes

censorship as "the suppression of ideas and information that some individuals, groups, or government officials find objectionable or dangerous" (ALA, 2019). Censorship of books can take two forms: overt and preemptive (Sachdeva et al., 2023). Overt forms of censorship include book bans and challenges. Preemptive censorship, also referred to as quiet or soft censorship, is when materials are deliberately removed, limited, or filtered out in the selection process before they reach students. This type of censorship frequently takes place within schools and ranges from administrations restricting book purchases, librarians filtering during the materials selection, and teachers removing books from curricula and classroom libraries. This removal of books is also referred to as self-censorship (Cooke & Harris, 2023). Although some types of soft censorship are categorized and delineated in the literature, this study revealed teachers' perspectives of how this censorship materializes within schools across the United States.

School Librarians and Soft Censorship

There is substantive research on censorship among librarians, and studies have exposed the prevalence of soft censorship in school libraries. *School Library Journal*'s 2023 Controversial Books Survey of school librarians showed that of the 729 respondents, the number of those self-censoring rose from 42 percent to 47 percent within the preceding year (Cockcroft, 2023), and 37 percent of librarians admitted that book challenges influenced purchasing decisions, 10 percent more than reported in 2022. They cited fears of parents, the community, and state legislation. The survey also revealed examples of quiet censorship from administrators. One participant noted that their principal, despite the librarian's protests, removed three books without following formal procedures. The books were later returned following public awareness of the censorship.

Principals can be key players in librarians' material selection. Dawkins (2018) surveyed 471 North and South Carolina school librarians to understand factors influencing their selection processes. She found that librarians who believed their principals would be uncomfortable with a potentially controversial topic experienced higher levels of discomfort, and in follow-up interviews, they shared that they chose to self-censor materials if they felt that their principals might be unwilling to back them in a challenge. In Carlson's (2020) survey of 446 K–12 American and Canadian public school librarians, 83.9 percent of respondents said they proactively censored texts due to content, and of these respondents, 70.5 percent self-censored due to sexual content and 17.6 percent for LGTBQ content. Relatedly, Tudor, Moore, and Byrne (2023) conducted a collections analysis of 90 Texan public high school libraries that excluded 55 controversial books to investigate how librarians might self-censor. They found that books with LGBTQIA+ content were less likely to be found in these school library collections. In a smaller survey of 18 Washington secondary school teachers and librarians, Daley (2020) also suspected that the participants reported they weren't experiencing censorship because of their self-censorship. For instance, two private school teachers noted that they pre-censored texts that were not age-appropriate or in alignment with Christian values.

These studies, taken together, demonstrate that school librarians are using forms of soft censorship, such as self-censoring, as a tool to respond to contextual pressures. An abundance of studies have focused on librarian soft censorship, and given the shared pressures librarians and teachers experience, we can posit that teachers may be experiencing similar pressures, yet studies related to practicing teachers are less common.

Teachers and Censorship

Empirical research demonstrates that censorship has been a persistent concern for teachers for decades, and their concerns largely echo themes of today—inconsistent levels of support from school leaders, community and parent pushback, and contention around curricular decisions (Agee, 1999; Donelson, 1969; Koss & Paciga, 2023b; Smith et al., 2018). With the rise in book bans and restrictive legislation around what can be taught in schools, recent studies have broadly explored teacher experiences on censorship.

First Book, a national education nonprofit, surveyed 1,501 participants from across its network of members who work in classrooms and programs that serve at least 70 percent children who come from low-income families (2023). Of these educators, 31 percent said they have experienced book bans, challenges, or restrictions in their school and/or district. Though a majority of educators noted not having experienced censorship, 46 percent of educators reported that the conversation around banned books already does or might influence the books they use in class, and 37 percent said it does or may influence the way they teach. Structural topic modeling of open-ended answers showed that most teachers (77 percent) engaged in self-censorship through buying fewer books, controlling distribution, and selecting texts more carefully. Also in response to censorship, 48 percent of teachers actively bought banned books for classroom use and 44 percent began teaching about the freedom to read. Of these responses, 25 percent noted how teachers followed administrative restrictions out of fear of losing their jobs.

Similarly, the RAND corporation through their 2023 State of the American Teacher Survey found that teachers were self-censoring (Doan et al., 2023; Woo et al., 2023). RAND surveyed 1,439 teachers from across the nation from their American Teacher Panel (ATP), a group of 25,000 K–12 public school teachers, in January and February 2023. Researchers found that 65 percent of teachers nationally decided to limit class discussions about political issues on their own without being directed by school or district leaders. The top three reasons teachers gave for self-censoring were uncertainty of leadership support if parents expressed concern, fear of verbal or physical altercations with parents, and fear of losing their jobs or teaching licenses. Teachers in conservative communities were more likely than teachers working in liberal communities to limit their instruction. Additionally, teachers in rural communities were less likely than urban teachers to oppose state restrictions. Of the teachers who were not subject to any local or state restrictions, 55 percent still decided to self-censor and limit their instruction about political and social issues, likely from spillover from other regions such as the 18 states in 2023 that restricted discussing issues of race and gender in schools.

Recent smaller studies have deeply explored teacher experiences and found similar results to the larger studies mentioned. Koss and Paciga (2023a) conducted a national survey of 503 preK- to eighth-grade teachers to investigate curricular freedom and censorship and found that teachers from the Northeast and the West were more concerned about issues of censorship at the national level, tended to reflect more liberal ideologies, and mentioned specific book bans attached to political issues. Teachers who criticized the far right were against censorship whereas those who criticized the far left were less against book banning. Meanwhile, teachers from the Southeast and the Southwest focused on individual, local, and state issues. The researchers posit that because those regions are more heavily Republican and Christian, they lead new legislation and gag-order bills for censorship, which aligns with teachers expressing more local concerns. Teachers in the Southeast had the most concerns with gender and sexuality content relative to other regions.

Focusing on a specific population, Pollock et al. (2024) conducted a study through a joint collaboration of scholars between New York University and the University of California San Diego to investigate the limitation effect (collective harm to learners through limiting access) of Florida restrictions across K–12 systems. They surveyed 76 individuals (48 educators and 28 community members) and conducted 13 semi-structured interviews with educators, parents, and students residing in Florida from April to June 2023. Respondents noted that the top three state regulations focused on limiting teaching related to sexual orientation, gender identity, and race and racism. A major finding was the approaches educators took to restrict books in libraries and classrooms. Books were removed from shelves and vetted for compliance with sometimes-overlapping state policies then potentially permanently removed books, or educators preemptively self-censored as a way to avoid potential punishment—even going as far as to remove entire classroom libraries. Other teachers no longer used books on specific populations or topics, such as books with queer characters, or limited student access to independent reading material.

In a recent smaller study, Sachdeva et al. (2023) investigated the self-reported experiences of censorship among seven teachers and school librarians from K–12 public schools. The researchers found that participants experienced varying levels of censorship, including an organization publicly targeting a text and a superintendent in another school removing a book from shelves without formal process. Some participants experienced social media vitriol and personal attacks whereas others had school and district support and were able to retain books after formal processes. Teacher experiences with censorship led to preemptive self-censorship. For example, after a public book challenge of Angie Thomas's *The Hate U Give* in one school, teachers refused to teach the book for fear of backlash, even though the novel was retained. Similar to studies with school librarians, this study describes multiple cases of soft censorship across the seven teachers' schools with little regard to official policies.

The studies of teacher censorship mirror the concerns expressed by librarians. Teachers are worried about issues of censorship at the local, state, and national levels and have experienced the impact of these measures in various forms from very public book challenges to quiet censorship from district officials and pressure to self-censor. Our study expands Sachdeva's (2023) work about soft censorship to a larger-scale analysis of the phenomenon. Like the larger studies mentioned, we sought to better understand instances of censorship, but we were more focused on soft censorship and the secondary English language arts teacher rather than all content areas. This study differs from those described above because it did not rely on convenience sampling with a subset of teachers from a specific state or organization but sought to invite all secondary English educators with a larger, more national sample to seek the largest representation possible.

Methods

This chapter is part of a larger survey measuring teacher experiences with diverse literature and censorship. The survey combines 32 original Likert-scale, multiple-selection, and open-ended questions. Items were generated from existing literature, surveys, and the theoretical frameworks of multicultural education and critical literacy (Banks, 1993; Lee & Low, 2017; Lewison et al., 2002; Gill, 2000; Stallworth et al., 2006).

We used the National Center for Education Statistics' (NCES) database to identify public US secondary schools (grades 5–12) and identified secondary English language arts teachers whose school websites posted their email addresses (N=107,605). From January 2023 to June 2024, we sent a 25-minute survey through Qualtrics and Gmail to all of the teachers. After eliminating incomplete and duplicate responses, 4,096 responses remained across all nine US geographic subdivisions, as divided by the national census (Table 1). Respondents taught in suburban (48.0 percent), rural (30.3 percent), and urban (21.7 percent) areas. Most taught at public schools (94.7 percent), followed by public charters/magnets (5.2 percent).

Participants' school economic statuses ranged, with most teachers working with lower middle-class populations (30.9 percent) followed by middle class (26.7 percent) (Table 2). Teachers predominately taught grades 9–12 (69.9 percent) followed by grades 6–8 (25.9 percent) and multiple levels from 6–12 (4.2 percent).

Among all responses, 43.7 percent of teachers (N=1,791) noted that their school, library, or district had engaged in censorship. This study analyzed these teachers' open-ended responses to the subsequent follow-up question: "Which title(s) or topic(s)? Who censored the title(s) or topic(s)? What was the reason provided?" During the analysis of this question, which focused on book titles and justifications, we saw a consistent pattern of teachers sharing instances of soft censorship within their schools and school libraries. This emergent pattern led to our research question: *How do teachers describe the ways that soft censorship appears in their schools and district?*

Open-ended questions were analyzed using Braun and Clarke's (2006) methodological approach, because no large national studies focusing on soft censorship exist. Rather than aligning with a preexisting theoretical framework, we sought to follow the data to

Table 1: Geographic subdivision

Geographic Subdivision	N	Percent
New England	215	5.2
Middle Atlantic	317	7.7
East North Central	485	11.8
West North Central	470	11.5
South Atlantic	871	21.3
East South Central	193	4.7
West South Central	506	12.4
Mountain	561	13.7
Pacific	478	11.7
Total	4096	100.0

Table 2: School economic status

School economic status	N	Percent
Lower class	953	23.3
Lower middle class	1265	30.9
Middle class	1093	26.7
Upper middle class	653	16.0
Upper class	126	3.1
Total	4090	100.0

identify frequent, dominant themes of soft censorship among the teacher responses. We independently (re)read all of the data and developed marginal, initial codes. These included paraphrasing teacher responses and in vivo codes (Saldaña, 2013). We were seeking patterned responses contextualized within the raw data and checked for consistency across our interpretations as we moved the initial codes into overarching themes (the Findings subheadings).

Findings

Findings revealed four teacher-described themes of soft censorship in their schools: a lack of transparency as to which texts were removed and the accompanying justifications for these text removals; preapproved lists, permissions, and purchasing as tools to block texts; solo insiders wielding power to quietly deny access to texts; and teachers and librarians avoiding texts to sidestep potential controversy. Within the findings, we aimed to highlight many voices within each section to show the breadth of experiences within each theme across the thousands of participants. We include the home states of the teachers to demonstrate the consistency and pervasiveness of these experiences across the US rather than to reflect the experience of that region of the country.

Soft Censorship as Intentionally Hidden and Lacking Transparency

Teachers described the myriad ways that censorship was opaque, lacking transparency of removed titles, justifications, and/or processes. Hundreds of teachers shared that they knew texts *had* been removed, but titles or justifications were not shared with them. For instance, a teacher from rural Texas described, "There has been a complete lack of clarity on which books were removed, who asked the board member to remove them, and why they were removed." A teacher from urban New Hampshire wrote, "I am not certain of the titles, but our librarian has been told to remove books from the library quietly." Teachers described the ways in which books were silently removed from classrooms, libraries, and the literal hands of the students without explanation. A teacher from rural Arkansas said, "Our AP Language and Composition textbook, without a school board hearing, 'disappeared' because a single parent complained that the book had a liberal agenda. No actual reasoning was provided as the books were never officially pulled; they just disappeared from classrooms and were retrieved from students." Often, teachers only knew about book censorship if they were actively teaching the text in question. A teacher from suburban Louisiana wrote, "They quietly censor books so it is difficult for me to make a list. I know they censored *Monster* by Walter Dean Myers because they literally came to my room asking for copies, but that's what they do. They take books out without officially announcing anything." The teachers understood that although there were public book bannings across the US, censorship was also occurring in the dark, avoiding detection.

Other hidden acts of censorship felt more nefarious in their intentions. Teachers described swaths of missing titles and calculatedly vague or deceitful justifications. A teacher from urban Missouri described,

> I do not know all the titles, but many students have complained about not being able to find authors or books that we have offered previously. The censorship

> was due to "explicit scenes." However, I do not know what definition of "explicit" was used, either, to determine this. Basically, the other reason is the school fears being sued over having these books available in the library.

Teachers repeatedly shared vaguely supported reasons for removing texts, but many mentioned that these removals were not announced, and students were suspicious of titles disappearing from shelves. A teacher from rural Washington shared how these vague reasons reflect books on specific topics: "It is generally pretty quiet so I don't know specific titles, but I know that books about LGBTQ issues and sexuality generally are hard to find." Given that texts with LGBTQ topics are overrepresented in challenges and bans, these texts were likely targeted to avoid controversy or even the attention that would have been generated following due process.

Several teachers wrote about large text removals concealed behind literal closed doors. A teacher in suburban Texas shared, "We do not know. Our library was quietly closed for three days while 'inventory' was taken. Books were removed, but we were not told anything," and a teacher in rural North Carolina wrote, "The library was closed for almost a week in order for there to be maintenance, but after speaking with the librarian, I found out they were removing books." Although quiet, these acts of censorship were described as methodical and substantial in their text removal. In rural Kansas, a teacher described books that had been "'in review' for multiple years now." The teachers' presumption was that the books would not be returned. The processes were conducted in a way that worked to subvert their memories of the books' very existence.

Soft Censorship through Preapproved Lists, Permissions, and Purchasing

Teachers described the ways schools utilized preapproval processes to shadow intentional book banning—an approach a rural Texan teacher called "sneaky censorship." Another rural Texan teacher outlined an approved text list separated by grade level: "So, thousands of texts have effectively been banned" by not making it onto the list. From rural California, a teacher wrote, "We have a short list of approved books, so everything else is pretty much banned by default, so definitely nothing LGBTQ allowed." In urban Oklahoma, a teacher wrote about an innately political process: "I know the selection process for library books is a form of censorship because it caters to the very conservative values of the community as a whole without taking into account the minorities within the community. Therefore, to my knowledge, no book has been removed because the book was never in the collection to begin with."

The lists were short and rigid, with many teachers noting their arrival following the recent rise in censorship efforts nationally. In rural Georgia, a teacher described that this required list "was not previously the case." Further, many teachers, such as one in suburban Nevada, wrote that attempts to get new books on the list were unsuccessful: "Everything suggested by me [is declined]. We need to stick to the textbook (even though students aren't reading it)." Similarly, an urban Washington teacher wrote, "Mostly censorship is de facto rather than de jure—we know we won't get a book about a topic approved, and so we don't even try." These preapproved lists frustrated teachers, who understood the motives, which served to barricade specific topics. Classical texts weren't immune from censorship, as noted by a teacher in rural Texas, who explained that *Romeo and Juliet* was

> de-listed (perhaps not banned outright) out of concern for young readers having examples of disobeying parental expectations by the titular characters. Sex, suicide, or bawdy word-play were not among the reported reasons to my knowledge, which makes the rationale seem like a veil for an agenda not explicitly shared with the public education system.

Other long-established classics also fell under the censors' gaze, including those by Shakespeare, Steinbeck, Orwell, and Dr. Seuss.

Some schools were described as having strict, almost draconian rules. When asked which books were banned, a suburban Florida teacher replied, "All of them. We are not allowed to supplement or replace materials. Students are not allowed to check books out of the library. This is Florida." These contexts were laden with rules and policies. As a teacher from suburban Arizona wrote, "Essentially, my district has committed censorship by exclusion by requiring all texts taught to be on an approved list from the school board. Controversial texts are conveniently left from that list, and teachers are frequently reprimanded for teaching texts that do not appear on that list." These restrictive lists effectively served as de facto censorship for any titles not explicitly named.

Beyond lists, schools across the nation required teachers to implement new book processes and permissions. An urban South Carolina teacher wrote that they must "register every book in our classroom libraries, and each one has to be read by three teachers" and in urban Ohio, a "very recent development" from the "latest election" is that all books must be approved prior to library purchase. This teacher anticipated potential classroom implications: "I don't know how this will develop or translate to my classroom." Beyond registering books, some schools were requiring permission slips and excessive procedures that made using new books a vexing inconvenience for already overworked teachers. In rural Georgia, a teacher wrote this made "the teaching of anything potentially controversial problematic with extra letters home and permission slips." A teacher in suburban Texas: "They had a lot of meetings claiming that they did not censor books, but they used soft censorship to remove them from circulation while librarians checked them. And adding the extra work onto teachers to send letters home if they teach 'questionable material' is just another way to censor diverse texts by giving us one more thing we don't have time for." Permission slips extended across both required and independently chosen books for students. In rural Arizona, a teacher shared, "Free-choice books students read on their own were censored a couple of years ago. Even if the book is free choice, teachers now have to pass out permission forms and have parents sign off that they know which book their child is reading. Teachers' individual libraries became 'risky liabilities,' according to the district."

Accompanying these strict rules and preapproved lists were rules and efforts that limited the acquisition of new texts. A teacher in urban Ohio described their experience how a specific title was "subtly censored when I asked my principal for permission to teach the book and purchase it." When students in rural California asked their teacher to learn more by reading books by Che Guevara, their teacher recounted that their administrator "said it was too politically biased and to get the money back for the books we ordered, even though the students asked to learn about Che." Purchasing was used in schools to prevent student access to appropriate texts, which resulted in increasingly dated collections. In rural Pennsylvania, for instance: "Our librarian has not been allowed to purchase any new YA or adult books in two years. This is because we are currently in the process of rating every book in the library, which isn't a good reason but is the reason given." In urban Virginia, a secondary teacher described censorship resulting in an "elementary school library," and in urban Ohio, a teacher wrote, "Our librarian hasn't been able to order new or replace existing books in our library." Bogging school librarians down with restrictions, overwhelming rating systems, and policies against new texts all served to bolster soft censorship.

Soft Censorship by an Individual with Power and Access

Teachers described how a single person in their schools held immense power to stealthily commit soft censorship. A teacher in rural Indiana described a veiled threat from two administrators: "My superintendent and curriculum and instructional design specialist informed me that we were not 'banning' the book, and I was not to use that word in regard to the situation. I was to tell anyone who asked that we as a department looked critically at our novel choices and chose as a department not to teach the book anymore." The teacher was ordered to lie by these two administrators in order to conceal their soft censorship. Librarians were described most in connection to solo acts of soft censorship. A teacher from suburban Texas wrote, "I saw *Persepolis* on a cart of culled books, among other teen books with sexual content or queer characters. I'm not sure if the librarian decided to cull the books or was directed." Others shared how their school librarian committed soft censorship acts independent of higher directives. A teacher from urban Alabama described a librarian who had "censored many titles that do not align with her personal beliefs"; an urban Oklahoma teacher described "a librarian who is very Christian and very conservative, and she will not stock a book that in any way addresses human sexuality—of ANY kind"; and an urban teacher from Minnesota described a librarian who "self-edits the collection in our library based on her own value system."

Some teachers expressed sympathy for their school librarians making "difficult choices," as described by a teacher in urban Kentucky, due to contentious contexts and uncertain job security. A suburban teacher in South Carolina wrote that her librarian, "pulled books she knew were banned elsewhere just to keep any issues from coming up at our school." Their soft censorship was sometimes described as necessary, as in rural Kentucky: "Our district parents are politically red and racist. *The Hate U Give* is kept behind the library desk and only recommended to certain students. The librarian told me this is how she keeps her job." Some participants expressed great frustration with their librarian culling books from their school library, as described by a teacher in suburban Kansas: "She did not have the authority to make the request." Yet other participants, particularly in conservative contexts, conveyed an understanding of their librarian's positioning.

These gaps in classrooms and libraries also impacted programming. A teacher in urban North Carolina wrote about the termination of their Battle of the Books program and although the school cited "disinterest," the teacher's "quick Google search" of the texts revealed the more likely reason connected to one text. The teacher surmised that the questioning of one book discontinued the entire program for 25 county schools—effectively banning the book along with all others within the program. Along with programs, healthy functioning school libraries disappeared. A teacher in urban Indiana wrote, "So many titles have been soft-banned, we no longer have a library. The reasons vary but often stem from promoting child independence and immorality." Students' ability to find a range of choices to read is described as an increasingly extinct reality.

Soft Censorship in Text Avoidance

Data revealed that teachers self-censored out of fear or avoidance of potential controversy. A teacher in suburban Colorado wrote, "I know that the librarian has removed some books proactively so as to not get in 'trouble.' No one has made her do it." Other teachers described a sort of haphazard avoidance of texts. For instance, a teacher in urban Indiana wrote that texts were censored if they had "anything that parents 'might not like' like 'curse words.' Senior teachers recommended the censorship to 'avoid problems.'" Some teachers avoiding texts used the same disappearing metaphors from the previous finding. A rural Alabaman teacher wrote, "*The Lovely Bones* just sorta . . . faded away. The sexual violence." Lacking clear reasons and without announcement of the books' departures, students are left searching for texts that are seemingly lost. Self-censorship is a particularly soft form of censorship because the books retreat noiselessly into the background.

Self-censorship attached to fear ranged from apprehension to panic experienced by participants themselves or their fellow teachers. For instance, following a rural Wisconsin controversy related to the book *Speak* due to the sexual assault and the book *Twisted* for the domestic violence and attempted suicide, neither book "was officially removed from class." Yet this teacher relayed that their colleague subsequently "stopped using the books after they were challenged." Although the teachers were supported, they chose to avoid potential backlash, which parallels the uncertainty described by a suburban Colorado teacher: "We are just afraid to teach certain books." Perhaps most concerning are the ways teachers described the resulting atmospheres following censorship attempts. In urban Alaska: "LGBT topics books were pulled from one HS library in my district. In addition, several of the titles were not LGBT but regarded racial inequity. Books were returned after awareness was raised, but the whole event was horrifying." In rural New Jersey, where a book was pulled and later returned, a teacher shared, "There has been a chilling effect in terms of what the media specialist keeps on the shelves." These "horrifying" and "chilling" instances undoubtedly impact teachers and librarians and, as described, led to a form of censorship that is difficult to track but that results identically to more public acts: the book disappears or is no longer a viable option.

Discussion

A decade ago, the late Teri Lesesne, a professor renowned for advocacy of the right to read, described that book bannings begin as snowflakes but coalesce into icebergs. She wrote that the greatest threat to reading was the 90 percent of the iceberg that lurks unseen beneath the surface. The purpose of this study was to develop a stronger understanding of how soft censorship materializes and is maintained in the United States—to "lower our line of vision" on this dark and expansive form of censorship that rarely appears in media headlines (2014, pp. 77, 81). We asked participants to share book titles and accompanying justifications provided for censorship. We anticipated justifications like sex, violence, and sexuality as reported in public scholarship (Meehan et al., 2023), yet the teachers shared examples of censorship that felt just as premeditated and manipulative as public censorship. Their responses revealed the penetrating reality that soft censorship is present in all of the ridges, junctions, and corners of the nation.

Data from this study supports related scholarship, such as Koss and Paciga's (2023a) study of K–8 censorship and contributes to the field in its analysis of the expansive ways that soft censorship occurs in secondary schools. Teachers described the prevailing ways that books are silently removed, culled onto library carts, blocked from approved lists or purchase orders, and avoided to prevent controversy. Their stories reveal that these instances are difficult to track and subvert. This quiet approach allows censors to avoid controversy or attention but also evades accountability. Intentional or not, soft censorship diminishes students' right to read.

Data demonstrated that acts of censorship were deliberate. In some school systems, those in positions of power maneuvered bodies and closed spaces in order to quickly and quietly extract books. In others, teachers turned instead to teaching less controversial texts. Although some publications position librarians as "the sole witness" to others' acts of soft censorship (Auguste, 2013, p. 126), findings aligned with scholarship that demonstrates the ways librarians—along with teachers—were also the censors (Carlson, 2020). Some of these acts accompanied political value systems, but often, they were completed out of avoidance or fear. Much of the soft censorship, when justified by the participants, was in response to a directive or a contentious context. Sometimes the directive was specific to a text or topic, but often, it came in the guise of preapproved lists or extra work and policies serving to keep texts out of buildings. These censors served as "catalysts of inequity" in their schools (Cooke & Harris, 2023, p. 4), and although the efforts visually appeared passive in their approach, they directly impacted students, who were required to relinquish half-read texts, to walk away from locked library doors, and to search unsuccessfully for missing (removed) texts. Just as the teachers recognized the deceit, innocuous justifications were likely not believable guises for impacted students either.

Censorship is depicted by the media and politicians in intensely raucous, divisive statements. In Sachdeva et al.'s (2023) study, the teachers took "the heat" as they advocated for their students in the midst of different levels of censorship both public and quiet (p. 45). The teachers' mechanisms for leveraging professional ethics, school policies, and institutional knowledge offer insight into how educators approach censorship at all levels. Yet this article's findings demonstrate the magnitude of soft censorship along with the strategies censors quietly use to remove, or encourage removal of, books across the nation. The nuances of soft censorship approaches suggest that more research is needed to undertake these silent forms. Our hope is that this study will "sound the alarm" that Lesesne (2014) describes before the iceberg "sinks the ship of books and reading and writing and teaching." If school libraries continue to close and relevant texts reflecting students' identities are removed, students will lose not only their right to read, but they just may lose their desire to read completely.

This study received funding from multiple sources to pay student workers to assist in data collection. These include Colorado State University, the

National Council of Teachers of English, Penguin Random House, Macmillan, and Scholastic. The funders had no role in the study design, analysis, or final report.

References

Agee, J. (1999). "There it was, that one sex scene": English teachers on censorship. *English Journal, 89*(2), 61–69. https://doi.org/10.2307/822141

American Library Association. (2019, March 29). *Intellectual freedom*. https://www.ala.org/advocacy/intfreedom

Auguste, M. (2013). *VOYA's guide to intellectual freedom for teens*. VOYA Press.

Bachmann, A., & Tellez, A. (2023). The war on books: Parent and educator perspectives. *Study & Scrutiny, 6*(1), 65–76. https://doi.org/10.15763/issn.2376-5275.2023.6.1.65-76

Banks, J. (1993). Multicultural education: Historical development, dimensions, and practice. *Review of Research in Education, 19*(1), 3–49.

Bishop, R. S. (2012). Reflections on the development of African American children's literature. *Journal of Children's Literature, 38*(2), 5–13.

Boyd, A. S., Rose, S. G., & Darragh, J. J. (2021). Shifting the conversation around teaching sensitive topics: Critical colleagueship in a teacher discourse community. *Journal of Adolescent & Adult Literacy, 65*(2), 129–137. https://doi.org/10.1002/jaal.1186

Braun, V., & Clarke, V. (2006). Using thematic analysis in psychology. *Qualitative Research in Psychology, 3*(2), 77–101.

Carlson, C. (2020). The fear of retaliation: Proactive censorship by public school librarians. *Michigan Reading Journal, 52*(3), Article 4.

Cockcroft, M. (2023, April 24). *Book challenges are having a chilling effect on school librarians nationwide | SLJ survey*. School Library Journal. https://www.slj.com/story/Book-Challenges-Are-Having-a-Chilling-Effect-on-School-Librarians-Nationwide-SLJ-Survey

Cooke, N. A., & Harris, C. N. (2023). The softer side of censorship. *Journal of Intellectual Freedom & Privacy, 8*(1), 4–9. https://doi.org/10.5860/jifp.v8i1.7964

Daley, E. (2020). Book challenges and bannings: Young adult literature censorship in Yakima County secondary schools. *New Jersey English Journal, 9*, Article 4.

Dawkins, A. (2018). The decision by school librarians to self-censor. *Teacher Librarian, 45*(3), 8–12.

Dellinger, H. (2021, October 6) How did 400 Katy ISD parents get a book removed? Accusations of Marxism and "critical race theory." *Houston Chronicle*. https://www.houstonchronicle.com/news/houston-texas/education/article/Woman-whose-petition-led-Katy-ISD-to-cancel-16512034.php

Doan, S., Steiner, E. D., & Woo, A. (2023). *State of the American teacher survey: 2023 technical documentation and survey results*. RAND. https://www.rand.org/pubs/research_reports/RRA1108-7.html

Donelson, K. (1969). A brief note on censorship and junior high schools in Arizona: 1966–68. *Arizona English Bulletin, 11*(3), 26–30.

First Book. (2023). *Educator insights on the conversation around banned books*. https://firstbook.org/wp-content/uploads/2023/10/2023-Banned-Books-Survey-Results.pdf?utm_source=firstbook&utm_medium=blog&utm_campaign=bannedbooks-study

Gill, D. (2000). A national survey of the use of multicultural young adult literature in university courses. *The ALAN Review, 27*(2), 48–50. https://scholar.lib.vt.edu/ejournals/ALAN/winter00/gill.html

Koss, M. D., & Paciga, K. A. (2023a). Curricular freedom in the contemporary sociopolitical context of the United States. *International Journal on Social and Education Sciences, 5*(4), 760–786. https://doi.org/10.46328/ijonses.594

Koss, M. D., & Paciga, K. A. (2023b). Five sites of resistance against censorship: Middle school teachers speak. *Illinois Reading Council Journal, 52*(1), 24–33. https://doi.org/10.33600/IRCJ.52.1.2023.24

Lee & Low Books. (2017). *Classroom library questionnaire.* https://www.leeandlow.com/educators/grade-level-resources/classroom-library-questionnaire

Lesesne, T. (2014). Right to read: The tip of the iceberg. *The ALAN Review, 42*(1), 77–81.

Lewison, M., Flint, A., & Van Sluys, K. (2002). Taking on critical literacy: The journey of newcomers and novices. *Language Arts, 79*(5), 382–392. http://www.jstor.org/stable/41483258

Lopez, B. (2021, October 26). *Texas House committee to investigate school districts' books on race and sexuality.* The Texas Tribune. https://www.texastribune.org/2021/10/26/texas-school-books-race-sexuality/

Meehan, K., Friedman, J., Baêta, S., & Magnusson, T. (2023, September 1). *Banned in the USA: The mounting pressure to censor.* PEN America. https://pen.org/report/book-bans-pressure-to-censor/

Mitchell, K. (2023). They need our support: A high school administrator's perspective on book selections in the era of state-sponsored censorship. *The ALAN Review, 50*(3), 46–48.

Nam, R. (2023). Teacher use of diverse literature in secondary English language arts classrooms: District barriers and resistance strategies. *Study & Scrutiny, 6*(1), 1–20. https://doi.org/10.15763/issn.2376-5275.2023.6.1.1-20

Natanson, H. (2023, June 9). Objection to sexual, LGBTQ content propels spike in book challenges. *The Washington Post.* https://www.washingtonpost.com/education/2023/05/23/lgbtq-book-ban-challengers/

Pollock, M., Yoshikawa, H., Diaz, J., Richburg, A., Cox, B., Matschiner, A., Homan, E., & Mohammed Issa, A.-R. (2024). *The limitation effect: Experiences of state policy-driven education restriction in Florida's public schools.* New York University. https://steinhardt.nyu.edu/ihdsc/limitation-effect

Sachdeva, D. E., Kimmel, S. C., & Chérres, J. S. (2023). "It's bigger than just a book challenge": A collective case study of educators' experiences with censorship. *Teachers College Record, 125*(6), 30–59.

Smith, A. M., Hazlett, L., & Lennon, S. (2018). Young adult literature in the English language arts classroom: A survey of middle and secondary teachers' beliefs about YAL. *Study & Scrutiny, 3*(1), 1–24.

Smith (Pseudonym), B., & Banack, A. (2024). Resisting the chilling effect of censorship and scripted curriculum. *English Journal, 113*(3), 29–36. https://doi.org/10.58680/ej2024113329

Stallworth, B. J., Gibbons, L., & Fauber, L (2006). It's not on the list: An exploration of teachers' perspectives on using multicultural literature. *Journal of Adolescent & Adult Literacy, 49*(6), 478–489.

Tudor, A., Moore, J., & Byrne, S. (2023). Silence in the stacks: An exploration of self-censorship in high school libraries. *School Libraries Worldwide, 28*(1), 1–17.

Woo, A., Diliberti, M., & Steiner, E. (2023). *Policies restricting teaching about race and gender spill over into other states and localities: Findings from the 2023 State of the American Teacher survey.* RAND. https://www.rand.org/pubs/research_reports/RRA1108-10.html

Middle School Teachers' Perceived Autonomy over Curricular Materials in a Charged Sociopolitical Climate

KATHLEEN A. PACIGA
MELANIE D. KOSS

Over the last several years, censorship has been a frequent subject of news reporting with recent increases in book challenges and book bans. Baêta and Meehan (2023) documented two years of concerted efforts by parents, school boards, and state legislatures to censor and restrict access to children's and young adult books deemed inappropriate and have called it a continued and "mounting crisis of book bans" (line 7). According to the American Library Association, book challenges have been surging in recent years, with a 65 percent rise in challenges in 2023 compared to 2022 (ALA, 2024). In addition, in the first half of the 2023–2024 school year, there were over 4,000 instances of book banning, which is more than the total of the entire 2022–2023 academic year (PEN America, 2024). Since 2021, 42 states have formally recorded at least one book ban (Meehan et al., 2024). According to an April 16, 2024, report (Meehan et al.), book bans are continuing to speed up across the country, and they are happening across the country, regardless of state political affiliation.

Censorship instances are often recorded via number, challenges, and percentages, but behind each book challenge and ban are those impacted by the bans, including students, authors, and teachers. The Meehan et al. report (2024) noted that "resistance is rising, and the very students whose right to read is being challenged and the authors whose works are being censored are fighting back in creative and powerful ways" (lines 23–24). Less pronounced are the teachers, who each have their own narrative and experiences regarding the selection and inclusion of children's literature for their classrooms and curricula. Instances of censorship and an increase in restrictive legislation (Kelly, 2023), then, impacts teachers' autonomy over selecting books for their classrooms and curricula, and their voices are the ones not often heard.

On any given day, a preK–8 classroom teacher makes many decisions regarding how they assemble their materials for instruction in their English and language arts components of the school day. They utilize standards, assess student interests, consult curriculum pacing guides, and lean on resources that curate lists of books recommended for children as they plan for whole groups, small groups, read-alouds, and individual instruction. Federal, state, or local legislation and/or district-level policy often governs what teachers can do with respect to their autonomy in selecting children's literature for instruction or inclusion in their classroom libraries.

A teacher's autonomy exists across three constructs: capacity, self-direction, and freedom (Smith & Erdoğan, 2008). These constructs operate "within spaces constrained by institutional, interpersonal, and intrapersonal factors" (Jackson, 2018, p. 2). Capacity relates to how well equipped a teacher feels about their ability to select appropriate materials within their instructional context. Self-direction relates to a teacher's ability to select appropriate materials independent of outside influences, while freedom relates to the impact of outside influences, such as administration, curricular constraints, parent involvement, and/or or the sociopolitical environment. These constructs can be extrapolated to the control teachers have over selecting literature for their classrooms.

According to Irwin et al. (2022), today's students are becoming increasingly diverse. Bishop (1990) stressed the importance of books serving as mirrors, windows, and sliding glass doors to allow students to validate their identities and learn about others, promoting learning, empathy, and compassion. Teachers use their professional knowledge to select books for their students that are relevant, engaging, and representative of today's diverse world. However, internal and external factors, such as today's sociopolitical context of book challenges and legislation, constrain teaching professionals and work against initiatives to diversify classroom literature selections. For a teacher to design instruction that effectively leverages children's literature, it must serve the needs of students within the sociopolitical educational context. Thus, capacity, self-direction, and freedom are intertwined.

Research Questions

The research question guiding this qualitative study was: *What are teachers' perceptions about their autonomy, defined as capacity, self-direction, and freedom, in selecting children's literature for their curriculum, instruction, and inclusion in classroom libraries?*

Methods

The present study reports on interview data collected with twenty-two grades 6–8 teachers. The interviews were conducted as a follow-up to a previous national survey of teachers in the United States (Koss & Paciga, 2023a, 2023b).

Data Source

A semi-structured, open-ended interview protocol (Bogdan & Biklen, 2007) was utilized. This structure allowed opportunities for participants to address common themes and the conversation to flow naturally from topic to topic. Below is the list of questions utilized in the interview protocol.

Questions to Guide the Semi-Structured Interview Protocol

1. How much choice, or control, do you feel you have in selecting children's literature for your classroom?
2. How equipped do you feel to make choices regarding children's literature selections in your classroom?
3. How supported do you feel in your selection of children's literature in your classroom?
4. What role do you think parents, administrators, or members of the school board should have in the children's books included in your classroom?
5. Are there any recent events or experiences that impact your view on the topic

of teacher choice over children's books included in the curriculum?

6. What and why?
7. Is there anything else you'd like to share with us about the children's literature you or others can and do use in the classroom? Or can't and/or don't use?

In addition to these questions, each teacher provided demographic information regarding their gender, race, age, years teaching, grade level, and school type. Transcripts were produced for analysis.

Participants

Five teachers per region of the Unites States (Northeast, Southeast, Midwest, West, Southwest) were targeted. Teachers in the Southwest were resistant to being interviewed, resulting in a sample size of two from the Southwest and 22 teachers total in the full sample. Interviews were conducted via Zoom and recorded.

The majority of participating teachers identified as female, White, and non-Hispanic with some representation in White-Hispanic and Black groups. The mean number of years in the field teachers reported was just under 15, $\bar{x}$=14.91, SD=8.37. Teachers most commonly reported being 35–50 years old, $\bar{x}$=43.45, SD=7.66. Half (n=11) of the participating teachers indicated they were employed in a suburban district. Two teachers were employed in rural districts, and the remaining nine worked in urban contexts.

Data Analysis

Data analysis occurred in three phases. In phase one, researchers viewed five recorded interviews (one per region of the US) simultaneously to establish open codes, with discussion leading to consensus. Using Atlas.ti, a qualitative data analysis software, researchers worked through the five transcripts to apply the codes and verify whether any additional codes were needed. Forty-nine open codes were established at the conclusion of phase one, see Table 1.

In phase two, researchers each independently viewed and coded half of the remaining 17 interviews. As-needed, researchers met to (1) discuss any questions that arose, (2) clarify codes, and (3) confirm codes were functioning as established. For example, two separate initial codes were "job security" and "earning tenure" that were later collapsed. As another example, in our initial list of 49 open codes, there were separate codes for topics teachers identified as controversial, including "diversity," "LGBTQ+," "race," "sensitive topic (suicide)," "sexual content," and "stereotypes or inaccurate portrayals." Relationships among these codes and superordinate codes were established within Atlas.ti, and 18 new codes were added when warranted. As new codes were established, previously coded responses were revisited using the constant comparative method (Glaser & Strauss, 1967).

Phase three began after all 22 interviews, totaling 2 hours, 28 minutes, and 27 seconds of run time, were initially coded. Using Atlas.ti, codes were networked, grouped, and/or collapsed to identify emergent themes. These themes were then aligned to the three constructs of teacher autonomy: capacity, self-direction, and freedom. (See the previous list and Figure 1 for samples of the resulting collapsed coding trees.)

Written memos were recorded to document researchers' interpretations of the interrelated constructs of teacher autonomy per participant/case.

Findings

Several major findings emerged. Coded transcripts suggested there was some overlap

Table 1: Codes Established in Phase One of Data Analysis

Initial Codes (Alphabetical)			
Absence of Literature	Academic Intervention/ Assessment	Administration Initiated	Book Knowledge
Capacity	Capacity-Building Resources	Censorship	Challenge
Control	Curriculum	Developmental Appropriateness	District Approval
District Restrictions	Diversity	Engagement	Evaluating Books
External	External Gatekeeping	Flexibility	Freedom
Funding	Inappropriate Language	Independent Reads	Instructional Setting
Internal	Job Security	Legislation	LGBTQ+
Librarian Recommendation	Moral Gatekeeping	Need for Balance	Parent Restrictions
Political Stance	Priority	Professionalism	Race
Religion	Risk	Self-Direction	Sensitive Topic (Suicide)
Sexual Content	Stereotypes or Inaccurate Portrayals	Student Choice	Team Teaching/ Planning
Tenure	Time Constraints	Voice	What Student Needs
Whole Class Reads			

Figure 1: Sample of Coding Tree Related to Self-Direction

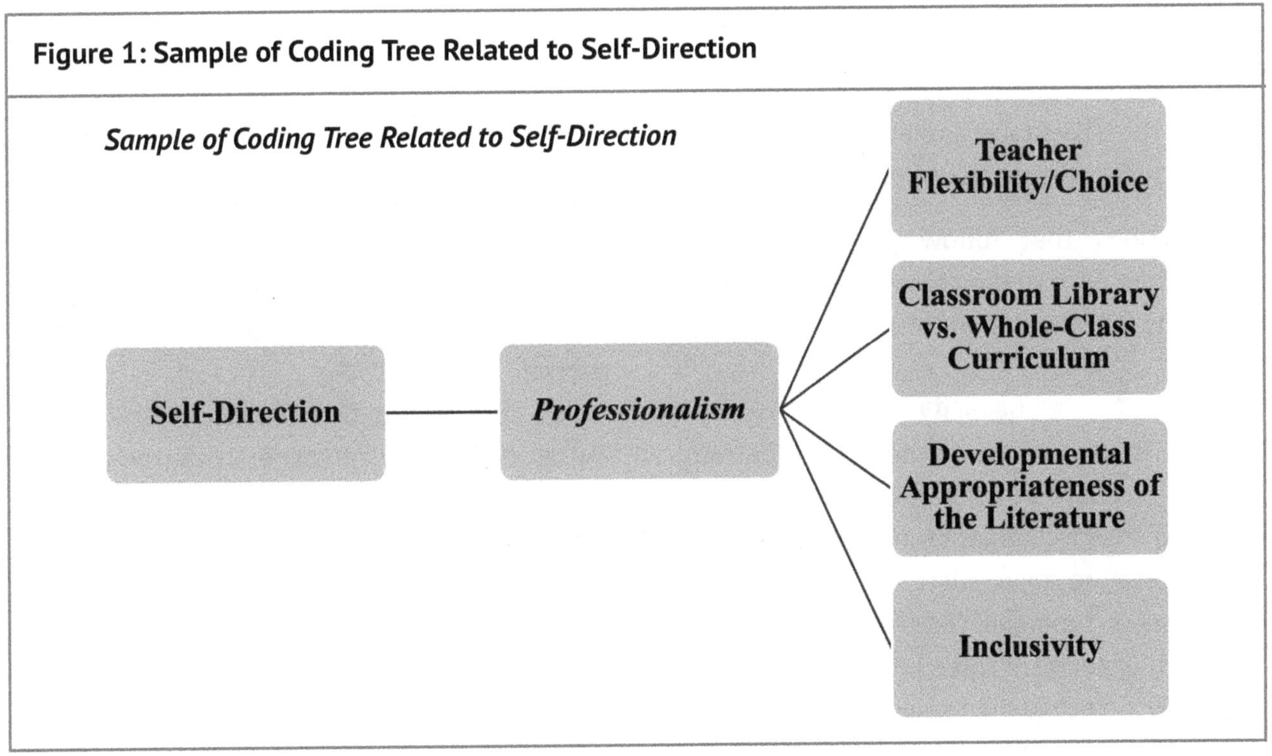

among the three constructs of capacity, self-direction, and freedom, as they are not conceptually distinct.

From the coding, it was clear most participants viewed themselves as highly capable. They reported teacher preparation experiences, professional reading, and collegial networking as ways they stay current on available literature. A common observed theme from this category was "I am well-prepared for this work." The constructs of self-direction and freedom were more nuanced, with several overlapping threads. Internal versus external influences impacted teachers' autonomy in varying ways. Key findings related to each construct of autonomy are presented below.

1. Teachers noted they felt a strong capacity for book selection.
2. Teachers utilized their experiences and outside resources to identify titles they deemed appropriate for their students.
3. Personal beliefs played a role in book selection.
4. Across all teachers, and regardless of overall state policies, the liberal or conservative makeup of the district in which they taught related significantly to their perceptions of freedom.

The sections that follow present example quotes from each of the components of teacher autonomy investigated in this study.

Capacity

Capacity is the knowledge needed to perform a certain action. Most participating teachers indicated they felt capable in their abilities to select literature appropriate for their students. Five themes emerged. Teachers reflected on their own capacity in three key areas: (1) in the ways they identified themselves as avid readers; (2) in discussion of their strategies for learning more about the selection of current resources available; and (3) in reflection on students' needs.

In reflecting on growing their own capacity for book selection through being an avid reader one teacher declared:

> So, I've been teaching for almost 25 years, and I feel very equipped to make choices about what is read aloud, what goes on the shelves, and what literature we use as part of the curriculum. I just have lots of experience working with the diverse group of people, and I am a huge consumer of YA [literature] and middle-grade reader stuff myself. So I, you know, can assess the quality of the writing but also the content of the writing.

Another teacher brought their colleagues in as support for their own growth in capacity: "My friends are all book nerds, so we talk books all the time." In addition, teachers also identified ways they utilize key industry resources to grow their capacity for selecting literature. One teacher reported, "I just read constantly, I read about different awards. I keep up with National Book Award, Newbery, and Goodreads Choice Awards, *[The] New York Times* bestsellers. I put a lot of time into keeping up to date on what popular books are."

In considering their capacity for addressing students' needs, teachers referred to their students' reading or developmental levels and their students' interests in and engagement with specific topics and titles:

> Usually, I will start with the data that I have on students as far as Lexile levels

> and reading levels. I also do a student interest survey to see, to try to get titles that are going to fit the needs of what I'm trying to teach and still be engaging for the kids, because I really want to try to draw them in. And you kind of have to walk a fine line there with what is going to be super-engaging for them and what's going to be best for what you're trying to do in the classroom.

Considering students' needs and interests is connected to teachers' reflections regarding the self-direction component of autonomy.

Across these examples, it was evident teachers felt they were capable of selecting books based on their current identities as readers. They reflected on the individual needs of their students and classrooms and, in doing so, felt capable and secure in their knowledge of existing resources as well as their ability to seek out additional resources as applicable.

Self-Direction

In order to effectively orchestrate students' learning in the English/language arts classroom, many teachers felt they needed opportunities for self-direction in their curriculum and instruction. Self-direction is a teacher's ability to select appropriate materials for teaching and learning *independent* of outside academic influences.

Consistent in the data was a theme of professionalism. Teachers resoundingly declared they know their students and provided commentary around four main areas related to self-direction: (1) teacher flexibility/choice; (2) classroom library versus Whole-class curriculum; (3) the developmental appropriateness of the literature; and (4) inclusivity.

Teachers reported some level of autonomy in terms of how much flexibility and choice they have regarding children's literature selections. On the one hand, a teacher proclaimed, "There's a lot of leeway given to our professional judgment." On the other, a teacher's response to one of the interview questions "How supported do you feel in your selection of children's literature in your classroom?" indicated some parameters surrounding their self-direction. She stated, "I'm free right now until I get in trouble."

Self-direction for book selection was indicated to a greater degree in the classroom library context compared to the selection of books to be used as part of the whole-class curriculum:

> In terms of my classroom library, however, I have total autonomy. I can put what I want, and I've recently this year, thanks to Donors Choose, put a lot more diverse books on my shelves: books by LGBT authors, African American authors, Hispanic authors, Asian and Pacific Islander authors, Muslim authors. I think I'm forgetting one group, but I tried to intentionally make my library as diverse as possible.

The teacher here was contrasting her library selections with those for the novels assigned for whole-class reading, which required district approval and team selection. In these cases, there was far less self-direction in the book selection processes.

Self-direction was amply evident in how teachers discussed the developmental appropriateness of specific books. In these comments, many teachers considered the degree of emotional intensity of the content in titles as well as their own perceptions regarding what students of a particular age can handle. As an example:

> I'm not going to put a book in front of a child that is going to be incredibly graphic or, you know, expose them to things that are inappropriate for an eleven year old. But, you know, children who are eleven can handle reading *Maus* (Spiegelman, 1986) and learning about the Holocaust. One book that we taught when we used to do class novels, one that our students loved, was *Roll of Thunder, Hear My Cry* (Taylor, 1976), and you know there is some stuff in that book that is really hard to take, but it's also good for them to see the world as it was so that they can make a better world in the future.

Analysis also indicated teachers' perceptions regarding what is controversial as well as their perceptions regarding anticipated or experienced community pushback shaped their self-directed selections for texts. This was true in the English/language arts classrooms as well as in content areas. One teacher who taught both ELA and biology indicated, "I avoid anything controversial. So, for example, I also teach eighth-grade biology. I do not discuss, and we completely skip over the chapter on, for example, sexually transmitted diseases. It's just . . . they're thirteen. They're thirteen."

Finally, teachers reflected on the relationship between their want for inclusivity and their self-direction-in-action regarding building their children's literature collection and selections for instruction. Many participants expressed the idea of mirrors and windows (Sims Bishop, 1990) in their interviews: "I kind of reflect that windows and mirrors philosophy and that my students do see themselves reflected in the books that we choose." In this vein, many teachers expanded beyond the metaphor, providing explanations for why they believe prioritizing diverse literature is important:

> We certainly are developing our curriculum around certain aspects or topics, but we do hope that we reflect characters who have different experiences so that a kid can see themselves reflected or use [a book] as a window into an experience that maybe isn't their own but might be their friend's or someone else around them, so that they can develop some empathy.

In addition to believing they were capable of selecting children's books, teachers believed they were professionals trained in teaching methods and should be able to select relevant and appropriate materials. They knew the curriculum, available resources, and their students' needs. Although they had differing levels of autonomy, teachers reported they made the best decisions possible to meet their classroom needs. They reported having more leeway on books they selected for their classroom libraries, and they made concerted efforts to include inclusive, developmentally appropriate books into their instructional spaces.

Freedom

This section explores how much control teachers feel they have over choosing materials for instruction or as components of their classroom libraries. It examines how external factors, like requirements from administrators or the state, limit this perceived control or freedom.

Two tensions related to freedom emerged from coding the interview transcripts. First, teachers expressed that some of the tensions surrounding their freedom emanate from personal, or internal, conflicts whereas others felt tension from external sources. Second, teachers tended to take either a censorship or an anti-censorship stance regarding their perceptions of curricular freedom. Within these tensions, three themes emerged from the data regarding freedom. These included moral gatekeeping (with awareness of outside pressures); opening doors (inclusion regardless of outside pressures); and parent or district influences providing either support/approval or restrictions for curricular and instructional decisions.

As an illustration of teachers' awareness of outside pressures and their enactment of moral gatekeeping on account of these pressures, a teacher from a school district that has been sued several times over book content shared, "I do think there is some hesitation on my end at times. I don't want to be in the center of that. You know, it gives me pause sometimes, just putting something on my shelf before I read it." In the subsequent thought, the teacher indicated she is fearful of oversight from the district and so chooses to not put questionable titles on the shelves in her classroom.

The second theme of opening doors also highlights the tensions teachers felt. In this code, teachers resisted restrictions to their freedom via censorship efforts. Several participating teachers reported they felt it was even more important to put diverse texts in their classroom as students might not see diverse texts elsewhere, especially in times of censorship. An example of this thinking drew upon Sims Bishop's (1990) metaphor teachers leveraged in their thinking about self-direction as well:

> It [censorship] definitely makes it even more important to have choice, to have a diverse classroom library where students not only see themselves but gain empathy by reading about the lives of people that you know they don't look like. We talk a lot about windows, mirrors, and sliding glass doors. That's a really important perspective that we take in my room.

In addition, teachers perceived their tenure status as securing their position and so felt empowered to open doors for students:

> Going forward, I will be putting more diverse books in my classroom because, well, I'm tenured now. I think that it's really important for kids to see themselves in books. I am teaching a more diverse class this year. It just is so apparent to me that having books that kids can relate to is so, so important for them, for their reading, for their personality development. So I will continue to do that, but I'm less worried about it now, even though politically I think [censorship has] gotten worse.

Parents and district administrators also played important roles in teachers' perceptions of their freedom. Their support and approval or restriction of children's literature for instruction or in the classroom library represented the last two themes related to freedom. A teacher thinking through her perceptions of district-level support for her freedom indicated:

> Our district has done a really great job of saying, "Hey, as a teacher, you do not need to be afraid of your [book] selections. If you think it's good for what you're doing right now, great. We'll support you if something comes up." And if you've gone, "Oh, gosh, maybe we

> shouldn't do this one," they encourage us to have some backups and to think about other alternatives. It is okay to take risks and try something different, so it's a beautiful situation we're in.

Teacher perceptions of support or approval were not reported universally, though. Many participating teachers shared concerns regarding the ways parents and the district administration restricted their freedom to select books for their classroom and instruction. One teacher specifically indicated the book approval process was too time consuming and did not allow for expeditious decisions regarding books following the summer months of curriculum planning. Another teacher reported concerns over the parent reactions to diverse representations in books she used:

> I actually have multiple books with LGBTQIA characters. I had a particular student at the beginning of the year who came out to me and asked for books with representation, so I handed them a few books over the year. The parents found out they were reading books with LGBTQ characters and demanded that I remove all books with LGBTQ characters from my classroom library. They went all the way to the superintendent to try to get me fired.

Fear of job loss or parent-initiated actions against them was common in the transcripts. For example, a teacher wanted to teach a specific text and opted not to, stating they were too nervous. We asked what they thought would happen if they had gone ahead with their text selection. They replied, "My guess? If a student complained to a parent, and that parent was the type to want to take it further, that they would . . . I don't know that I'd be supported for my choice."

Overall, the teacher participants reported varying aspects of freedom in their autonomy over selecting children's literature and curricular materials. The idea of freedom appeared in the data as an individualized construct tied to teachers' own set of moral values, alongside the influence of external factors such as the sociopolitical environment and related national discourse around censorship. Teachers wanted to uphold their personal convictions related either to the inclusion or exclusion of diverse and inclusive titles while navigating the community and district influences and requirements.

Discussion

The middle school teachers interviewed in this study reflected the varied environments in which they teach and the flexibility or restrictions of the curricula and literature they include in their instruction and their classroom libraries. All the teachers valued children's literature and its place in the classroom. They felt competent and capable of selecting literature and in their abilities as teachers. They desired the ability to self-direct and believed autonomy is essential if they are to meet the needs of their students. However, there were varying realities regarding their freedom to choose children's literature. Regardless of where they personally fell on the political spectrum, almost all of them were against overt censorship and book bans, even if they personally served as moral gatekeepers over the books they selected for their classrooms. Essentially, these teachers believed they were professionals and were trained to select appropriate books for their classrooms and students.

In many states, preservice teachers study

children's literature as a component of their licensure programs. They are taught methods for aligning book selection to disciplinary standards and to the needs of their students. Many inservice teachers are expected to use provided curricula that has children's literature included; others have provided curriculum and are given leeway or encouragement to add supplemental texts, and yet others have more flexibility in curriculum and text selection. Depending on context, some teachers have more autonomy than others to select texts based on their learned knowledge of practice and student needs. In this work, a one-size-fits-all approach is not applied.

Proposals and actions toward implementing one-size-fits-all curricula and sets of children's literature emanate from a context in which teachers' and students' realities may be highly politicized, sometimes oppressive, sometimes overly inclusive, and filtered by personal, local, and/or state-level biases (Koss & Paciga, 2025). Regardless of state or district, legislation and news surrounding censorship and book banning impacts all teachers. Teachers are responsible for teaching their students, and trust in teachers and public education is essential for teachers to feel safe and competent in doing their jobs.

The impact of educational gag orders and censorship initiatives, whether promoting the restriction of certain titles or topics or pushing for inclusion of certain issues and topics, impacts teachers' abilities to feel safe and supported in their book selections and, in turn, their jobs. Teachers reported feeling capable and confident in their ability to select appropriate books for their students, yet teachers have also reported feeling that their jobs are on the line, and this can inhibit their willingness to take risks. As a result, some teachers are reporting self-censoring and not taking risks so as not to get in trouble and/or lose their jobs (Najarro, 2024). As noted by PEN America (Friedman et al., 2023), restrictive legislation has exerted "new control on public education by intimidating educators into self-censoring, taking a wide berth around any topics that could incur controversy or conflict," topics that may align with or go against a particular teacher's personal beliefs.

The legislation and increased emphasis on censorship and control over what books and topics are allowed in educational spaces also impacts students, both in terms of what books they are exposed to and how safe they might feel in schools. If a teacher's ability to select curricular texts and to curate and build classroom libraries is restricted, students, in turn, have access and exposure to vastly different sets of books and content depending on where they live. If books with LGBTQ+ content, for example, are banned in schools and districts, then students who identify as members of the LGBTQ+ community may feel unwelcomed, marginalized, and in some cases be in danger, as they are explicitly targeted in some legislative texts. This can be a vastly different experience for students who attend a school in which LGBTQ+ identities are welcomed, promoting an inclusive community. If the goal of education and learning is to create students who are active and valued citizens and who will ultimately make society a better place, then what they are taught in school is vitally important. Books have the potential to teach students who they are and where they fit into the wider world—serving as mirrors, windows, and sliding glass doors (Bishop, 1990).

Implications

As Freire (1968) suggested, "All education is political; teaching is never a neutral act" (p. 19). Internal and external influences will inevitably impact teachers' autonomy and curricular freedom. In today's political climate, a study of teachers' perceived autonomy over the books they include in their classrooms sheds light on how teachers feel about their professionalism and rights in the classroom. Teachers have indicated they feel as though their professional freedoms are being constrained—curricular silencing—in many places in the US. Connecting the ideal of curricular freedom to contemporary reality provides an overview of the interconnectedness of teaching and the role teacher autonomy can have on the educational system. An understanding of how teachers perceive their freedoms helps us as teacher educators understand how to assist teachers in understanding the significance of and fighting for curricular freedom.

References

American Library Association. (2024, March 14). *American Library Association reports record number of unique book titles challenged in 2023.* https://www.ala.org/news/2024/03/american-library-association-reports-record-number-unique-book-titles#:~:text=Breadcrumb,titles%20were%20targeted%20for%20censorship

Baêta, S., & Meehan, K. (2023, December 14). *Spineless shelves: Two years of book banning.* PEN America. https://pen.org/spineless-shelves/

Bishop, R. S. (1990). Mirrors, windows, and sliding glass doors. *Perspectives, 6*(3), ix–xi.

Bogdan, R., & Biklen, S. (2007). *Qualitative research for education: An introduction to theories and methods* (5th ed.). Pearson.

Freire, P. (1968). *Pedagogy of the oppressed.* Bloomsbury Academic.

Friedman, J., LaFrance, S., & Meehan, K. (2023, August 23). *Educational intimidation.* PEN America. https://pen.org/report/educational-intimidation/

Glaser, B. G., & Strauss, A. (1967). *The discovery of grounded theory: Strategies for qualitative research.* Aldine.

Irwin, V., De La Rosa, J., Wang, K., Hein, S., Zhang, J., Burr, R., Roberts, A., Barmer, A., Bullock Mann, F., Dilig, R., & Parker, S. (2022). *Report on the condition of education 2022* (NCES 2022144). National Center for Education Statistics. https://nces.ed.gov/pubsearch/pubsinfo.asp?pubid=2022144

Jackson, D. O. (2018). Teacher autonomy. In J. Liontas (Ed.), *The TESOL encyclopedia of English language teaching* (pp. 1–6). John Wiley & Sons. https://doi.org/10.1002/9781118784235.eelt0221

Kelly, L. B. (2023). What do so-called critical race theory bans say? *Educational Researcher, 52*(4), 248–250. https://doi.org/10.3102/0013189X231159382

Koss, M. D., & Paciga, K. A. (2025, in press). Teacher autonomy and decision making on curricular book choices. *Reading Horizons: A Journal of Literacy and Language Arts.*

Koss, M. D., & Paciga, K. A. (2023a). "We have to be wary of unicorns and rainbows": Curricular freedom in a contemporary sociopolitical context. *Literacy Research and Instruction,* 1–25. https://doi.org/10.1080/19388071.2023.2293689_

Koss, M. D., & Paciga, K. A. (2023b). Curricular freedom in the contemporary sociopolitical context of the United States. *International Journal on Social and Education Sciences, 5*(4), 760–786. https://doi.org/10.46328/ijonses.594

Meehan, K., Baêta, S., Markham, M., & Magnusson, T. (2024, April 16). *Banned in the USA:*

Narrating the crisis. PEN America. https://pen.org/report/narrating-the-crisis/

Najarro, I. (2024, February 15). Teachers censor themselves on socio-political issues, even without restrictive state laws. *EducationWeek*. https://www.edweek.org/teaching-learning/teachers-censor-themselves-on-socio-political-issues-even-without-restrictive-state-laws/2024/02

PEN America. (2024, April 16). *New report finds unprecedented surge in school books bans*. https://pen.org/press-release/new-report-find-unprecedented-surge-in-school-books-bans/

Smith, R., & Erdoğan, S. (2008). Teacher-learner autonomy: Programme goals and student-teacher constructs. In T. Lamb & H. Reinders (Eds.), *Learner and teacher autonomy: Concepts, realities, and responses* (pp. 83–102). John Benjamins.

Spiegelman, A. (1986). *Maus: A survivor's tale*. Turtleback Books.

Taylor, M. D. (1976). *Roll of thunder, hear my cry*. Dial.

Challenging Times: Book Challenges and State Consolidation of Power in South Carolina

SUSAN CRIDLAND-HUGHES
JENNIFER GALLMAN
JED CRIDLAND-HUGHES

Since 2019, book challenges have proliferated in the United States with book-banning activity reported in 42 states since 2021 (Friedman, 2022; Meehan et al., 2024). Book-banning efforts have not only increased geographically but also in volume—PEN America, an organization dedicated to tracking book banning, highlights that "the bans are speeding up. There were over 4,000 instances of book bans in the first half of this [2023–2024] school year—more than all of last school year as a whole" (Meehan et al., 2024). Most important, the PEN report identifies shifts in public policy as one of the structural changes adding fuel to the book-banning fire. States are passing additional legislation criminalizing conversations about diversity, equity, and inclusion in public spaces (Adams & Chiwaya, 2024).

In South Carolina, decisions regarding instructional and supplementary materials have long been left up to local control through the policies of the school boards of individual districts. This has led to a wide range of policies regarding procedures for challenging materials in schools and to a difference in outcomes of challenges based on the demographics of districts and policies governing the composition of challenge committees. However, as rhetoric surrounding censorship of educational materials escalated at a national level, the variety of procedures for challenging items inherent to a localized system came to be seen as a potential liability. State legislators and the State Department of Education sought to centralize control over school and library materials in an iterative process of layering in which new, restrictive policies were added to proposed legislation, ultimately making it unwieldy. Ultimately, the process devolved such that "power passes from those affected, or citizens in general, to classes of experts able to manipulate information and representation of issues, stifling dialogue and popular involvement in decision-making" (Lo Bianco, 2001, p. 224). Centralized restrictions on reading materials passed in South Carolina in a manner that was profoundly undemocratic, and new restrictions have led to confusion and concern among local school districts as they seek to reconcile their local procedures and policies.

This study focuses on where policy power rests and who controls the policies that control curricular freedom.

Critical Race Theory and Critical Policy Analysis

We situate this study in the landscape of analyses of attacks against K–12 schools accused of teaching critical race theory (CRT). CRT argues that racism is "ordinary, not aberrational" (Delgado & Stefancic, 2001, p. 7) such that systems that appear objective are still enmeshed with racialized assumptions. For educational researchers, then, CRT becomes a lens through which to explore "issues of school discipline and hierarchy, tracking, controversies over curriculum and history, and IQ and achievement testing" (Delgado & Stefancic, 2001, p. 3). The 1619 Project was published in 2019 as a website and educational materials designed to "reframe the country's history by placing the consequences of slavery and the contributions of black Americans at the very center of our national narrative," immediately sparking backlash from conservatives across the country as an example of CRT infiltrating schools (*New York Times Magazine*, n.d.; Muir & O'Keeffe, this volume).

We focus specifically on battles over books as curriculum. As schools expand the texts they use, external groups attack the diversified curriculum and create restrictive policies to protect/fortify the status quo. These challenges themselves could be seen as evidence of the very concepts taught in the CRT framework, as "part of a movement to sustain a system in which Black, Brown, and the white poor are miseducated and undereducated in an increasingly carceral public school system and state" (Greene, 2021, p. 267).

We also view the data collected through the lens of critical policy analysis (Apple, 2019). Critical policy analysis views policies (defined broadly) as artifacts of society, where "the politics and compromises that go into the creation of a policy, and the preferred meanings that are contained within it, need to be critically examined" along with "how the policy is distributed and given authority and power" and how that policy is "received, reinterpreted and even resisted" (Apple, 2019, p. 280–281). Apple argues that expanding neoliberalism in education creates a politics of, among other components, "privatization, attacks on teachers and teacher unions . . . a climate of White supremacy, [and] a culturally restorative project to reinstall what is assumed to be high status knowledge in schools" (2019, p. 277); he also, however, emphasizes the "outside-to-inside" connections that shape our schools. It is those "outside-to-inside" connections that we focus on here. We look at how policy layers shape responses to book challenges, where federal rhetoric, strategy, and policy map onto state-level policies and local efforts to both attack and defend schools.

Choi and Seon describe policy layering as "how a policy keeps its core purpose by adding new layers in response to political pressure for more substantial changes" (Choi & Seon, 2021, p. 598). They also highlight how "tense layering," or layering affected by conflicting pressure from different groups, can, in fact, make the final policy inconsistent (2021). Using this frame as our model, we look first at the federal level to identify the signals that allow for the attacks on schools. We then move to our specific focus on South Carolina, highlighting state-level legislation and organizational restructuring that centralizes power in the state. Finally, we look at one example of a local district and how the policies become more targeted to support the prevailing political structure rather than becoming more resilient, as well as one counter-example in which a policy was recently revised to be more protective of students' right to read at the local level and was countered at the state level.

The Evolution of the Current Book Challenge Movement

In September of 2020, then-president Donald Trump signed Executive Order 13950: Combating Race and Sex Stereotyping. This executive order stated that "it shall be the policy of the United States not to promote race or sex stereotyping or scapegoating in the Federal workforce or in the Uniformed Services, and not to allow grant funds to be used for these purposes. In addition, Federal contractors will not be permitted to inculcate such views in their employees" (Executive Order 13950, 2020). The first column of Table 1 indicates the portions of the EO 13950 that directly relate to identifying and defining the "divisive concepts" in the bill.

EO 13950 was an immediate signal that federal policy had shifted away from foregrounding the assumption that the United States should attend to potential discriminatory actions related to race and sex. Although the Biden administration revoked EO 13950 in January of 2021 (Executive Order 13985, 2020), EO 13950 had already signaled to state-level actors how to create restrictive policies tied to the notion of "divisive concepts." EO 13950 offered a framework for states to write legislation attacking tenets perceived to be aspects of critical race theory. While an exploration of how this emerged in all states is beyond the scope of this chapter, we will discuss the divisive concepts language specific to the attacks on diversity, equity, and inclusion in South Carolina.

Outside of the federal legislative and executive space, national conservative think tanks also provided model legislation for states seeking to make schools more "transparent." The Manhattan Institute, specifically, provided language for legislation that required schools to post all curricular materials for review by the public at large in response to the divisive concepts policy (Manhattan Institute, 2021). Section 2 reads:

> SECTION 2. TRANSPARENCY IN TRAINING AND CURRICULUM
>
> A. The governing body of a public school, including public charter schools, shall ensure that the following information is displayed on the school website in an easily accessible location:
>
> (1) All instructional or training materials, or activities, used for staff and faculty training [OPTIONAL: add "on all matters of nondiscrimination, diversity, equity, inclusion, race, ethnicity, sex, gender, or bias, or any combination of these concepts with other concepts"].
>
> (2) All learning or curricular materials, or activities, used for student instruction [OPTIONAL: add "on matters of nondiscrimination, diversity, equity, inclusion, race, ethnicity, sex, gender, or bias, or any combination of these concepts with other concepts"]. (Rufo et al., 2021)

This model proposed that all learning materials be provided prior to the beginning of the class, without allowance for deviation from the transparency requirements. The optional elements reveal that the focus of the model legislation is to expose any elements in which schools may consider identity and diversity within the context of the classroom. When combined with concurrent legislative attacks on diversity,

Table 1: Comparison of specific elements of Executive Order 13950 (2020) and the South Carolina Integrity and Transparency in Education Act, H. 5183 (2022)

Executive Order 13950	S.C. H. 5183
Divisive Concepts	
one race or sex is inherently superior to another race or sex;	one race, sex, ethnicity, color, or national origin is inherently superior to another race, sex, ethnicity, color, or national origin
an individual, by virtue of his or her race or sex, is inherently racist, sexist, or oppressive, whether consciously or unconsciously;	an individual, by virtue of the race, sex, ethnicity, religion, color, or national origin of the individual, inherently is privileged, racist, sexist, or oppressive, whether consciously or subconsciously;
an individual should be discriminated against or receive adverse treatment solely or partly because of his or her race or sex;	an individual should be discriminated against or receive adverse treatment because of the race, sex, ethnicity, religion, color, or national origin of the individual;
an individual's moral character is necessarily determined by his or her race or sex;	the moral character of an individual is determined by the race, sex, ethnicity, religion, color, or national origin of the individual;
an individual, by virtue of his or her race or sex, bears responsibility for actions committed in the past by other members of the same race or sex;	an individual, by virtue of the race or sex of the individual, bears responsibility for actions committed in the past by other members of the same race, sex, ethnicity, religion, color, or national origin;
meritocracy or traits such as a hard work ethic are racist or sexist, or were created by a particular race to oppress another race.	meritocracy or traits such as a hard work ethic: (a) are racist, sexist, belong to the principles of one religion; or (b) were created by members of a particular race, sex, or religion to oppress members of another race, sex, ethnicity, color, national origin or religion.

equity, and inclusion practices in publicly funded spaces, the neutrality of transparency shifts into a targeted attempt to expose schools for violating new and/or pending legislation. This pending legislation would not exist without a signal at the federal level that DEI initiatives were no longer protected.

Uptake of National-Level Rhetoric in South Carolina

Our focus on South Carolina highlights what we see as an evolution of the attacks on books and curriculum. From 2021 to 2023, the South Carolina legislature unsuccessfully attempted to pass legislation that would restrict access to reading materials related to the divisive concepts framing. Ultimately, the failure of the legislature to enact a law in this area led to a change in strategy, and the state's Department of Education, now led by a radical conservative superintendent, stepped in to create policy that bypassed the legislature.

In April 2022, the South Carolina House of Representatives introduced H. 5183, the South Carolina Transparency and Integrity in Education Act. This bill mirrored much of the language present in model bills, stating that certain concepts could not be included "in a course of instruction, curriculum, assignment, instructional program, instructional material (including primary or supplemental materials, whether in print, digital, or online), surveys or questionnaires, or professional educator development or training" (SC Transparency and Integrity in Education Act, 2022). As seen in Table 1, much of the language from the federal Executive Order 13950 was reproduced in the proposed state bill, almost identically, indicating that the rhetoric at the national level had, indeed, filtered down into more local legislation.

As mentioned previously, backlash against the 1619 Project and CRT led many conservative politicians to include language in bills such as the one in South Carolina that were specifically directed at prohibiting the use of educational materials from the project; hence, the bill also prohibited "instruction or instructional materials which create a narrative that the United States was founded for the purpose of oppression, that the American Revolution was fought for the purpose of protecting oppression or that United States history is a story defined by oppression" (SC Transparency and Integrity in Education Act, 2022). Additionally, the bill created a requirement for school districts to create a mechanism for parents, students, and employees of a school district to file complaints regarding potential violations of the proposed law and requirements for resolving those complaints.

While the bill passed the House, it did not make it out of committee in the Senate before the end of the legislative session. Sponsors reintroduced the bill in the following session in January of 2023 as H. 3728 (SC Transparency and Integrity in Education Act, 2023). Once again, the bill passed in the House, with a new amendment that gave parents the right to sue school districts for violations of law, "without regard to whether the person commencing the action has sought or exhausted available administrative remedies" (SC Transparency and Integrity in Education Act, 2023). After this amendment proved a sticking point for some senators, the bill did not clear a conference committee designed to create a compromise bill between the House and the Senate, failing to pass for a second year in a row (Reynolds, 2024, p. 5).

With a second failure in 2022, proponents of censorship began to seek other avenues by which to restrict access to diverse educational materials. Meanwhile, South Carolina elected a new Superintendent of Education, Ellen Weaver. Weaver had previously served as the CEO of a conservative think tank, the Palmetto Promise Institute, and campaigned against diversity in education, saying "she wanted to keep 'woke Washington ideology' out of South Carolina classrooms" and that "critical race theory was 'everywhere' in America's education system" (Flynn, 2024, p. 1). In September of 2023, the State Department of Education officially published notice of proposed Regulation 43-170, Uniform Procedure for Selection or Reconsideration of Instructional Materials. Past legislation focused on restricting texts related to "divisive concepts," but Reg. 43-170 primarily focused on restricting sexual content in books. While this ostensibly again was "neutral," these restrictions often remove texts with LGBTQ+ characters and texts by authors of color. Up until this point, local school districts had the freedom to create their own procedures for selecting education materials, as well as hearing and adjudicating challenges to those items, and had been updating local policies.

Under Reg. 43-170, the State Board of Education can determine the appropriateness of any materials available in schools, either as part of the curriculum or in libraries, and any decisions made by the State Board are binding on all districts in the state, regardless of where the challenge originated (Uniform Procedure for Selection or Reconsideration of Instructional Materials, 2023). Additionally, the regulation states that "the State Board may, but is not required to, of its own volition and on its own initiative, make determinations regarding the educational suitability or the Age or Developmental Appropriateness of specific Instructional Materials pursuant to the criteria and requirements of this regulation" (Uniform Procedure for Selection or Reconsideration of Instructional Materials, 2023). Beyond the adjudication of a challenge process emerging at the local level, the regulation allows for the unilateral removal of resources by the State Board of Education.

This regulation bypassed the standard legislative approval process; the proposed regulation was sent to the South Carolina Assembly in February of 2024, at which point the legislature had 120 days to provide input on the rule. However, neither the House nor the Senate ever discussed the proposed regulation during the session, so the bill became official at the end of the legislative session in May (Jurado, 2024, p. 2A). In both bills proposed in the Assembly, the legislature's inaction made it such that laws restricting educational materials did not become law. However, the State Department of Education exploited that same inaction to get a regulation enacted that placed the power to restrict materials across the entire state in the hands of the State Board of Education.

Over 380 authors of children's and young adult books teamed up with publishers and advocacy groups to send an open letter to South Carolina legislators after the passage of Regulation 43-170 (PEN America, 2024). Major publishing companies like Macmillan and Penguin Random House, advocacy groups such as the ACLU of SC and We Need Diverse Books, and leading authors Ellen Hopkins and Laurie Halse Anderson signed the open letter. South Carolina resident and author Jessica Khoury, who has a daughter in the state's public school system, signed the letter initiated by PEN America with concern over a student's right to a "full and comprehensive education" (O'Toole, 2024) should the regulation go into effect, especially with broad language that could be applied to many books. In tense layering, the final enactment of a policy often obscures more than clarifies; in this case, the enacted policy gives schools little guidance on what can be challenged, creating an even stronger sense of fear for people teaching and learning in those spaces.

Local Resistance against Policy Layering and Control

We started our research by tracking how pending legislation at the state level was affecting individual district-level policy, creating a spreadsheet with a list of all school districts in South Carolina, locating publicly available policies for that board in 2021, and tracking how three local school boards changed their process in response to public pressure (Cridland-Hughes & Cridland-Hughes, 2022). However, much of what we tracked is undercut by the consolidation of power at the state level.

Local advocacy has been present since the beginning of the current national book ban movement, with mixed results (Hixenbaugh, 2024). In South Carolina, grassroots and local advocacy efforts fought against and continue to challenge both state-level consolidation and more restrictive local policies. These efforts include students and parents, and, in individual situations, teachers. On February 13, 2024, while

Reg. 43-170 was still in legislative limbo, the South Carolina Board of Education held a meeting in which Superintendent Weaver told the students in the audience that they were misled about her policy. In a video posted by the ACLU of South Carolina, several students remarked about what is "best for students," referring to the policy as "seven pages of nonsense" and referencing James Madison's *The Federalist Papers* to argue that factions are a danger to the inclusive whole, ultimately questioning the Board's responsibility to students (ACLU of South Carolina, 2024).

Some of South Carolina's high school students and parents have organized as pro-literacy advocates. Most locally known is Beaufort County's Diversity Awareness Youth Literacy Organization (DAYLO), which received a national commendation from the American Association of School Librarians (AASL) in March 2024. Founded by student Holland Perryman in 2021 after 93 books were challenged and removed from the Beaufort High School library, DAYLO has been a prominent voice in student advocacy for intellectual freedom ("DAYLO Honored," 2024) with established chapters at high schools throughout the state. Other South Carolina advocacy groups include Freedom to Read SC and ProTruthSC, both of which organize through social media. Freedom to Read SC, supporting South Carolinians' First Amendment rights, was established in 2022 and includes "educational organizations, civil rights groups, religious entities, and others" (ACLU of South Carolina, 2022). The ProTruth SC Coalition, a grassroots organization composed of the E3 Foundation, the Lowcountry Black Parents Association, the ACLU of South Carolina, and the NAACP Legal Defense Fund, is primarily focused on diverse and inclusive history (ProTruth SC, n.d.). And parents are speaking out against book removals; one Beaufort parent stated (Beaufort County Board of Education, 2023):

> I am the Reverend Lori Gorgas Hloppin. I serve the Unitarian Universalist Fellowship of Beaufort located on Ladies Island. At home, I have about a dozen copies of a book . . . that might be found in some of your homes and maybe even in the schools of this district. However, some of these books, themes are disturbing: incest, rape, murder, explicit sex. In one story, two young women get their father drunk in order to have sex with him. This is after that same father had offered the young women to an angry mob to be raped . . . . As a parent and a pastor, I support parents being involved in their children's education and monitoring what their children are reading and viewing. What I cannot support is one person or one small group of people making the decision of what will be available in libraries and classrooms for all the families in a school district. I urge the board to return all the books that have been removed from the library shelves and classrooms now. Let our educators and librarians teach, let our parents make literature choices appropriate for their own families not other families . . .

Reg. 43-170 went into effect without any official legislative vote (Markham, 2024). Even though there was some pushback against the policy, SC Superintendent Ellen Weaver did not waver in her belief that books should be censored for sexually explicit content and, in fact, funded a lobbyist to shepherd the regulation through the adoption process (Ingalls, 2024;

Jensen 2024). Teachers have mostly remained silent on the passing of Reg. 43-170, but one of the most concerning elements of the regulation is the vague language in the bill. Palmetto State Teachers Association member and lobbyist Patrick Kelly explained that teachers will have difficulty interpreting the new guidelines because of the regulation's ambiguous rhetoric, adding unnecessary stress to teachers who already feel scrutinized (Frost, 2024).

Concluding Thoughts

Our hope in beginning this research two years ago was to track how local districts and advocates either resisted or reinforced restrictions on books. We noted that applicable policies occur at multiple levels, starting at the federal level with Executive Order 13950 from September 2020 then moving to the state level with legislation both enacted and proposed. The instructional challenge process and the supplemental materials adoption process both previously occurred at the local level, even if challengers are using resources provided from a nationwide conservative organization. It is worth noting that many of the district-level policies indicate that decisions about materials will be made by professional teachers and librarians but emphasize that the superintendent and/or principal has ultimate authority for the adoption of materials in the classroom.

What we did not anticipate was how much local control over education would be sacrificed to the idea of absolute curricular control. External forces pressure policy: in SC, this includes state think tanks like the Palmetto Family Council, local chapters of national organizations such as Moms for Liberty, the South Carolina School Board Association, and the governor. There are also counterbalances in the form of local community groups, the ACLU, coalitions, NCTE Book Rationales, and the courts. Policies have some malleability, but that seems to be only minorly important at this point. In many cases, policies are ignored in favor of secretly removing books that appear on externally created lists.

Resistance is key: teachers and supportive parents have been instrumental in identifying the attempts to secretly remove books from classrooms. Students have had the most success in South Carolina in pushing back against local attempts to ban books. As South Carolina is a right-to-work state, teachers have focused less on group organizing and more on individual acts of resistance while also relying on private coalitions with parents that allow for advocacy. There have been some successful examples of resistance; in Beaufort, 92 out of 97 challenged books were returned to school library shelves (Pelley, 2024). However, the decisions to keep those books were made by book review committees at the local level. That procedure may no longer be relevant, as the state regulation now allows for another level of appeal.

The policies governing book bans and book challenges are constantly in flux, and, in SC specifically, changes in personnel can determine how stringently they are adopted. The election of Ellen Weaver as State Superintendent of Education has resulted in 1) a state-level book review committee and policy, 2) the stacking of political hirees and appointees supportive of restrictive book adoption policies, and 3) the severing of existing relationships with professional associations supporting librarians. The consolidation of power at the state level means that districts attempting to put in place guardrails to challenges can be overruled. It also means districts are anticipating guidance from the state level before making decisions specific to the desires of their local constituents.

Returning to the idea of policy learning and

policy layering, South Carolina is an example of what we consider a policy hydra—as challenges to a poorly thought-out policy emerge, the conservative group trying to consolidate control learns and adjusts, and two new heads of attack emerge. The layers of policy in South Carolina now mean that work done at the local level (for Beaufort, the work includes the process to evaluate 93 challenged texts, both in terms of community investment in the book challenges committees and in the actual cost to taxpayers to facilitate the challenge process) is subsumed by a regulation that was never discussed in the public record by elected officials. The question remains as to how local advocacy efforts will adjust to the continuing restriction on the youth freedom to read, particularly regarding materials dealing with issues of race, gender, and sexuality. What we report here is the current state of policies and procedures in South Carolina, but more restrictive policies have been proposed and may be taken up in the next legislative session. The next front will likely be more extensive advocacy through the state and federal courts.

References

The 1619 Project. (2019). *The New York Times Magazine.* Retrieved September 13, 2024, from https://www.nytimes.com/interactive/2019/08/14/magazine/1619-america-slavery.html

ACLU of South Carolina. (2022, October 27). *Advocates launch "Freedom to Read SC" coalition to fight book bans across South Carolina.* https://www.aclusc.org/en/press-releases/advocates-launch-freedom-read-sc-coalition-fight-book-bans-across-south-carolina

ACLU of South Carolina [@aclusc]. (2024, February 16). *S.C. Education Superintendent Ellen Weaver told a roomful of students they were "misled" about her proposed book censorship policy* [Video]. Instagram. https://www.instagram.com/p/C3aSrq7PDvk/

Adams, C., & Chiwaya, N. (2024, March 2). *Map: See which states have introduced or passed anti-DEI bills.* NBC News. https://www.nbcnews.com/data-graphics/anti-dei-bills-states-republican-lawmakers-map-rcna140756

Apple, M. (2019). On doing critical policy analysis. *Educational Policy, 33*(1), 276–287. https://doi.org/10.1177/0895904818807307

Beaufort County Board of Education. (2023, January 17). *Beaufort County Board of Education board meeting* [Video]. BCTV. https://beaufortcountysc.new.swagit.com/videos/205894

Choi, T., & Seon, S. W. (2020). Target groups on the mainline: A theoretical framework of policy layering and learning disparity. *Administration & Society, 53*(4), 595–618. https://doi.org/10.1177/0095399720949853

Cridland-Hughes, S., & Cridland-Hughes, J. (2022, November 17–20). *Challenging times: Book challenges in the age of critical race theory* [Conference presentation]. National Council of Teachers of English Annual Convention, Anaheim, CA, United States.

DAYLO honored with national commendation. (2024, March 13). *The Island News.* https://yourislandnews.com/daylo-honored-with-national-commendation/

Delgado, R., & Stefancic, J. (2001). *Critical race theory: An introduction.* New York University Press.

Exec. Order No. 13950, 85 F.R. 60683 (2020). https://www.federalregister.gov/documents/2020/09/28/2020-21534/combating-race-and-sex-stereotyping

Flynn, H. (2024, January 21). Era of the political superintendent: Year ahead will shed light on Ellen Weaver's impact. *The Post and Courier.*

Friedman, J. (2022, September 19). *Banned in the USA: The growing movement to censor books in schools.* PEN America. https://pen.org/report/banned-usa-growing-movement-to-censor-books-in-schools/

Frost, J. (2024, June 27). *"Book banning" rule goes into effect in South Carolina schools.* WLTX News19.https://www.wltx.com/article/news/local/book-banning-regulation-goes-into-effect-sc-schools/101-705238f0-7c44-4aa1-85a0-7c11b92b7d24

Greene, L. S. (2021). Critical race theory: Origins, permutations, and current queries. *Wisconsin Law Review, 2021*(2), 259–268. https://wlr.law.wisc.edu/wp-content/uploads/sites/1263/2021/06/16-Greene-Final-.pdf

Hixenbaugh, M. (2024). *They came for the schools: One town's fight over race and identity, and the new war for America's classrooms.* HarperCollins.

Ingalls, C. (2024, April 2). *SC Superintendent of Education talks accomplishments, goals after first year in office.* ABC 4 News. https://abcnews4.com/newsletter-daily/ellen-weaver-south-carolina-superintendent-of-education-talks-accomplishments-goals-after-first-year-book-ban-regulations-teacher-pay-increase-letrs-program-literacy-rates-board-of-ed-support-teachers-april-2-2024

Jensen, K, (2024, June 18). *Two vague and dangerous book ban bills in South Carolina target public and school libraries.* Book Riot. https://bookriot.com/two-vague-and-dangerous-book-ban-bills-in-south-carolina-target-public-and-school-libraries/

Jurado, A. (2024, June 26).In SC, local school officials won't have final say on books bans. Who has the power? *The State.*

Lo Bianco, J. (2001). Policy literacy. *Language and Education, 15*(2–3), 212–227. https://doi.org/10.1080/09500780108666811

Manhattan Institute. (2021, December 2). *Manhattan Institute releases policy document for improving transparency in school training and curricula.* https://manhattan.institute/article/manhattan-institute-releases-policy-document-for-improving-transparency-in-school-training-and-curricula

Markham, M. (2024, May 10). *The state of book bans: South Carolina is poised to get worse.* PEN America. https://pen.org/the-state-of-book-bans-south-carolina-is-poised-to-get-worse/

Meehan, K., Baêta, S., Markham, M., & Magnussen, T. (2024, April 16). *Banned in the USA: Narrating the crisis.* PEN America. https://pen.org/report/narrating-the-crisis/

Muir, A., & O'Keeffe, J. (2024). The meaning of "informed American patriotism": Teaching the 1619 Project in Texas. In A. D. David, K. Covino, C. L. Dobbs, C. Emeran, & M. Letcher (Eds.), *The impacts of censorship, volume 1: Research on the intersection of censorship and teaching English* (pp. 47–54). National Council of Teachers of English.

O'Toole, J. (2024, June 7). *State book regulation poses threat to freedom, advocates say.* Statehouse Report. https://www.statehousereport.com/2024/06/07/book-banning-ap-course-quotes/

Pelley, S. (2024, March 3). *Beaufort, South Carolina, schools return most books to shelves after attempt to ban 97*. 60 Minutes. https://www.cbsnews.com/news/beaufort-south-carolina-schools-return-most-books-to-shelves-after-attempt-to-ban-97-60-minutes-transcript/

PEN America. (2024, June 6). *Major writers for children and young adults among over 380 authors calling on South Carolina lawmakers to reject restrictions to evaluate books in public schools*. https://pen.org/press-release/major-writers-for-children-and-young-adults-among-over-380-authors-calling-on-south-carolina-lawmakers-to-reject-restrictions-to-evaluate-books-in-public-schools/

ProTruth South Carolina. (n.d.). *South Carolina for truth in education*. Retrieved July 14, 2024, from https://www.protruthsc.org/

Reynolds, N. (2024, June 29). Bill banning "prohibited concepts" in SC public schools fails. Rare loss for conservatives. *The Post and Courier*.

Rufo, C., Copland, J., & Ketchum, J. (2021, December 1). *A model for transparency in school training and curriculum*. Manhattan Institute. https://www.manhattan-institute.org/transparency-school-training-curriculum

South Carolina Transparency and Integrity in Education Act, H. 5183, 124th Sess. (2022). https://www.scstatehouse.gov/sess124_2021-2022/bills/5183.htm

South Carolina Transparency and Integrity in Education Act, H. 3728, 125th Sess. (2023). https://www.scstatehouse.gov/sess125_2023-2024/bills/3728.htm

Uniform Procedure for Selection or Reconsideration of Instructional Materials, SC R. 43-170 (2023). https://ed.sc.gov/state-board/state-board-of-education/library-regulation/library-files/sbe-regulation-43-170/

The Meaning of "Informed American Patriotism": Teaching the 1619 Project in Texas

ALISIA N. MUIR
JAMES O'KEEFFE

A brief by the National Education Policy Center defines "discriminatory censorship laws" as "certain official acts that regulate classroom conversations about racism, gender identity, and other targeted topics" (2023). The same brief estimates that as of November 2023, enough states and school districts had enacted such laws as to affect the lives and education of about half the entire population of K–12 public school students in the United States. Meanwhile, campaigns to ban specific books from local school classrooms and libraries have accelerated in what PEN America has deemed an "Ed Scare," an apparent political backlash to two events: the initial publication of the 1619 Project in 2019 and the widespread racial unrest following the murder of George Floyd in 2020. PEN further reports that "[b]ooks about race and racism, and books with characters of color, were the targets of 37 percent of all book bans in the 2021–22 and 2022–23 school years" (Meehan et al., 2024).

The 1619 Project, an ongoing initiative of essays, poetry, and multimedia composed by a variety of authors and artists, was first launched by *The New York Times* in August 2019 to recognize the 400th anniversary of slavery's beginnings in colonial New England, and it seems to have been the main catalyst for the Texas legislation two years later. The state legislature meets each odd-numbered year, and so the 87th session that ran from January through October 2021 was the first to convene since the 1619 Project's initial publication. A letter co-signed by Texas Attorney General Ken Paxton and sent to the United States Department of Education in May, for instance, singles out the 1619 Project for promoting "factually deficient history" and "ahistorical concepts."

The impetus for our research was the aforementioned pro-censorship political climate in our home state of Texas. In December 2021, a law enacted by the 87th Texas Legislature aimed at curbing the alleged influence of CRT in public school classrooms took effect. Among other strictures, Senate Bill 3 specified that teachers "may not . . . require an understanding of the 1619 Project" (Texas Legislature, House 8). Although numerous challenges to specific book titles at the local level were common beforehand, this exclusion at the legislative level arguably constituted the first statewide book ban in Texas history, qualifying SB3 as the kind of discriminatory censorship law defined above.

In the same legislative session, lawmakers also approved House Bill 4509, which purports to require the teaching of "informed American patriotism" in K–12 schools through the use of primary-source documents such as the Declaration of Independence and *The Federalist Papers* (Texas Legislature, Senate 1). Both SB3 and HB4509 regulate social studies curricula throughout Texas, and at the time of this research, precise guidelines for implementing both laws in the classroom were pending review by both the Texas Education Agency (TEA) and the State Board of Education (SBOE).

The developments in Texas presented a unique challenge, and an opportunity, for English language arts teachers. Although neither of the new laws that govern the teaching of social studies and US history applies directly to ELAR instruction, the same political climate that fostered the 1619 Project ban would presumably be no more tolerant of ELAR teachers incorporating elements of the 1619 Project into their students' exploration of literature. Yet the official state curriculum standards, the Texas Essential Knowledge and Skills (TEKS), would seem to foster such exploration. Rule 7(A) of the subchapter that governs grade 11 ELAR, for example, requires not only that students "read and analyze American literature across literary periods" but also that they analyze both informational and argumentative texts. The "Inquiry and Research" strand for the same grade level expects students to locate, examine, and synthesize "a variety of sources" into an original research product. And regardless of grade level, authorities on best practice for teachers of English language arts, including NCTE and the National Board for Professional Teaching Standards, have long advocated interdisciplinary collaboration. It would therefore be reasonable for an ELAR teacher of high school students to consider the 1619 Project, with its variety of readily available resources, all of them centered on one of the fundamental concerns of United States life, history, and literature—the institution of slavery and its lingering consequences—when devising a curriculum that meets all the above expectations.

The research fellows proposed that the 1619 Project was a collection of primary sources, and we further agreed with NCTE's contention that "historical documents and artifacts—as well as images, social media posts, and videos created with contemporary technologies—all serve as primary sources, worthy of interrogation," as noted in its concurrent New Perspectives on Primary Sources (NPPS) Project. But if Texas teachers elected to circumvent legislation banning the 1619 Project by utilizing those resources, then what were the potential consequences, both short term and long term? Would teachers be sanctioned legally and/or have their licensure sanctioned? Should ELAR teachers in Texas assert the prerogative of assigning the essays, poems, and instructional materials published by *The New York Times* and the Pulitzer Center in association with the 1619 Project, especially given that Texas lawmakers had (as yet) placed no corresponding restriction on these materials within the state ELAR curriculum? Or would doing so be a needless provocation in an already politically charged teaching environment?

Methods

The US Geological Survey describes Texas as "the largest land area of any state in the contiguous United States" (USGS, 2021). The Texas Education Agency (TEA) is a state agency that oversees public education in Texas. Due to the state's size, the agency has divided Texas into twenty regional educational service centers. We investigated the following questions by documenting the ongoing effects of the new legislation within our educational service area, which comprises twelve independent school districts and eight charter school entities in West Texas. Specifically, we aimed to gather anecdotal evidence and teacher testimony that recorded:

1. Impacts of school-district resolutions regarding the 1619 ban.
2. How school administrators received and interpreted the legislation in order to apply it to the needs of their schools.
3. How classroom teachers received and interpreted the legislation and how their classroom practice changed.
4. Any resulting sanctions against ELAR teachers for violations of this HB at state and local levels.
5. How the legislation limits cross-curricular collaboration between ELAR and social studies teachers.

In addition to the anecdotal evidence, which we viewed as vital to documenting the experiences of English teachers in our region, we meant to develop guidelines that assisted Texas ELAR teachers who wished to support their social studies colleagues in helping students analyze the plethora of primary-source documents cited by the 1619 Project. Wherever possible, we wanted to document any attempts by ELAR teachers in Texas to incorporate the 1619 Project's original materials, including our own.

Request for Stories and Testimonies

We drafted a preliminary call for stories and sought contact with most if not all the ELAR teachers in school districts in the western region of Texas.

Questions to Gather Stories and Testimonies

1. Has your state passed legislation that impacts what you can teach?
2. Has your school district enacted a policy that impacts what you can teach?
3. Has legislation influenced what or how you teach your course?
4. Would you like to share anything else?

We used our professional contact lists asking K–12 school-based administrators, ELAR teachers, and librarians in our region if they were interested in participating in our survey. The researchers received 19 responses. Fifteen responses were a result of the initial request, and four were secondary responses gleaned by word of mouth from the original respondents. Respondents were given the choice to respond anonymously, via phone call, in person, or by email. The respondents fit into the following demographic:

1. One respondent was a high school administrator
2. One respondent was a district-level ELAR curriculum specialist
3. Three respondents were school-based librarians
4. One respondent was a retired high school ELAR teacher in an IB world school
5. Thirteen respondents were ELAR teachers

By May 2023, we had compiled enough stories to form a coherent narrative of SB3's effects on our region, and in November we presented our findings in a roundtable session at the NCTE Annual Convention in Columbus, Ohio.

Data Analysis

Our data management and analysis components followed the recommendations of Creswell and Creswell (2023). Appropriate data management means storing, coding, interpreting codes, and presenting findings to our audience in an ethical manner (Merriam & Tisdell, 2016). We utilized proper data management techniques, including collection, documentation, and secure retention (Maxwell, 2013). To ensure adequate data collection, documentation, and retention for this inquiry, we used computer-assisted qualitative data analysis software, such as NVivo15 by Lumiverro (Maxwell, 2013).

Open coding was used as an approach to analyze the testimonies and stories that were collected to obtain themes and then to categorize them based on the testimonies and stories provided by the respondents (Creswell & Creswell, 2023). We relied on a multifaceted approach such as finding synonyms and words with similar roots. We also connected similar concepts that were offered by respondents. Using this process, we were able to develop conclusions from the data.

Findings

School Systems' Resolutions

Researchers discovered that all school systems in the surveyed area were against Texas's SB3 and HB4509 on philosophical levels. All school districts proposed adopting measures to articulate their feelings and took measures to adopt formal resolutions. In each case, school boards underestimated the public response to those proposed resolutions. For example, one district entered 20 opposition emails into the public record of their school board meeting. The emails urged the district to support Texas's measures for varied reasons. One of the more popular reasons was that critical race theory was a "hateful and destructive ideology." Another reason was that the district "didn't have funding to include critical race theory into its curriculum." Another reason cited confusion as to the "district's motivation to enter a political arena, especially during COVID." All of the districts in the surveyed area deferred action on their resolution proposals in order to do more research on SB3 and HB4509 and to conduct public education and listening sessions; however, in each of the school districts, no further action was taken.

ELAR Classrooms Impacted

While the ban applied to the social studies classroom, it impacted ELAR classrooms, as well as librarians in K–12 schools. During the survey period, the following books were challenged in school libraries and ELAR classrooms in the survey area:

a. *The Perks of Being a Wallflower* (gender, LGBTQ, obscene themes)
b. *The Kite Runner* (sex, violence)
c. *Feed* (language)
d. *House Built on Ashes* (gender, LGBTQ)
e. *Gender Queer* (LGBTQ, sex, language)

Respondents shared that they saw an upward trend of parents challenging what books teachers had in their classroom libraries, as well as books that they chose to use as a part of their ELAR curriculum. School districts had varied approaches to handling parent challenges. We discovered that large school districts had procedural policies for how books would be challenged before they were excluded from libraries but relied on grade-level reading lists for selecting texts for ELAR classrooms. Smaller districts had library policies but navigated parental challenges in ELAR classrooms on a case-by-case basis.

ELAR teachers acknowledged that parents had the right to voice opinions on what their child could or could not read. One respondent shared, "I have school-aged children that attend school in the district where I work. I know what my kids can and cannot handle. If I think my child can't handle a particular subject being covered in a class, I am going to work with the teacher to navigate the issue." Teachers in the respondents' group said that they found it difficult to establish and maintain the balance between parental rights and exercising their own intellectual freedoms. To teachers, it appeared that parents were overstepping their rights to advocate for their children by asking districts to remove materials from schools for all students. Another respondent shared, "[Teachers] go to school and have lots of training. I have a master's degree. Parents say that we work hard and that they trust us to do what is best for kids, but then stuff like this happens, and I question if I actually have parent support."

Grant Writing

The researchers discovered that teachers and librarians in the surveyed area found creative ways to balance parent challenges while maintaining their intellectual freedoms. Survey respondents used grant writing, negotiation, and collaboration as leveraging tools. For example, a middle school librarian searched for outside funding sources and then had "my district's grant department help me complete applications and apply for a grant." Through a grant, the librarian was able to secure genres that were not available in the school's collection or were being challenged in the district.

Collaboration with Nonprofit Organizations and Institutions of Higher Learning

One researcher, a high school ELAR teacher, applied and was accepted into the Pulitzer Center's 1619 Project Afterschool Partnership. In addition to participating in a series of virtual professional development sessions, the partnership required educators to facilitate "at least one activity using resources from the 1619 Project during fall 2022 or winter 2023 with a group of students in their afterschool program."

This requirement presented a challenge, albeit a welcome one, to recruit students and to implement the activities in a school setting where the use of 1619 Project materials was expressly prohibited by state law. The partnership's requirement that each educator identify an established afterschool program within their professional community worked in support of this mission. After the campus administration granted tentative approval to proceed, the researcher approached the district's language services department, with whom they had collaborated on prior afterschool activities, and the department granted its support and sponsorship, providing personnel and bilingual dictionaries to help facilitate the after-school sessions.

The researchers then contacted the local community college, already an instructional partner with the high school, and asked permission to hold the after-school sessions at the college library, adjacent to but technically apart from the high school's campus. The head librarian volunteered afternoon use of the library's computer lab, seating up to sixty students, and relevant technical support for the lab's multimedia equipment.

Again with the approval of the high school administration, the researchers recruited student participants through their English classes and daily announcements that specifically appealed to students' curiosity. The daily announcement was, "What is the 1619 Project? Why is it banned in Texas schools?" Students voluntarily participated in three afterschool sessions between November 2022 and February 2023. Their responses to the initial exit surveys indicated increased awareness of the topics discussed, e.g. "[I learned] [t]hat the erasure of black history stems so much deeper than slavery. I had no idea even highway placements/systems divide and segregate groups of people"; "[I learned that] [t]he first slaves to be brought to the land of America were brought in 1619 shortly after the founding of Jamestown." All students who attended the first session answered "Very likely" to the question, "How likely are you to attend the next session?"

Follow-up sessions included a study of erasure poetry using an excerpt from the Fugitive Slave Act of 1793 and virtual visits with Pulitzer Center Reporting Fellow Irene Vázquez and documentary filmmaker Te Shima Brennen. For these latter two sessions, the researchers also coordinated with two extracurricular clubs, the campus chapter of Gay Straight Alliance and the creative writing club.

One District's Story

A small district's Curriculum and Instruction (C&I) department believed that Texas's social studies ban could be applied to ELAR classrooms. As a result, C&I worked with one of its high schools (going forward called "The Team") that had previously gleaned successful results with book challenges in their ELAR classes. That school's policy had been to handle challenges on a case-by-case basis. The operational procedures were fluid and were amenable, depending on the specific parent who was making a challenge. The Team used Google to locate various policy statements that addressed mature content for high school students, as well as examples of policy procedures for parents wanting to initiate book challenges.

The Team developed a two-pronged approach during the research period. First, C&I asked teachers in this school to include a statement in their course syllabus. This statement, adapted from the College Board, is called the PreAP Equity, Access, and Mature Content Policy. Secondly, a Challenge Request Form was developed and linked from each teacher's syllabus to the school's website. The form included a statement from the school on how its teachers selected educational texts for its ELAR classrooms, as well as a specific outline of the timeline for their challenge process.

The form asks parents to:

1. Provide their contact information
2. Describe the book being challenged (name, author, publisher, copyright date)
3. State if they have read the book (if they had not read the book but were familiar with it, they were asked to state what they knew about it)
4. Explain the nature of their concern (including page numbers or specific passages)
5. State what immediate action was being requested and if the action should apply to their child or to all children reading the book
6. Provide recommendations for alternate books that would accomplish the same educational objective as the book they were challenging

The policy was tested for the school year in order to give parents, teachers, and other stakeholders time to provide feedback on the policy once it was placed into effect. At the conclusion of the school year and the policy testing period, the school district leadership began the process of developing a district policy.

Going Forward

Texas ELAR teachers who wish to incorporate elements of the 1619 Project directly in their classrooms are limited to those elements that exist apart from the project's original content, such as historical documents and literary works referenced in the project's essays and online materials. Yet these materials are plentiful, ranging from photos of African American historical figures and events to musical recordings to the ongoing works of the journalists, poets, and historians who are among the project's contributors.

Teachers who wish to engage their students with the 1619 Project more directly also have a variety of options, most of which involve collaboration and partnership with other stakeholders in the community. Above all, student participation in any such initiatives must be voluntary. Teachers should approach their administrators early and with a plan that specifies the context of such activities, how students will be recruited, and any partnering organizations or entities. As noted earlier, there are a number of national programs that can help facilitate a teacher's efforts, such as the Pulitzer Center's 1619 Project Afterschool Partnership. However, given the current and unique intellectual climate in Texas, teachers are also advised to form local collaboratives that build support and appeal to the needs of their respective communities before launching any such efforts.

Extracurricular programs offer the best potential context for these initiatives. Creative writing, art, and drama clubs can delve into the project's original poetry, literary fiction and nonfiction, music, and illustrations, for instance. Academic competition groups like Quiz Bowl and Destination Imagination can study and deconstruct the project's essays. And ELAR teachers can take advantage of their cross-disciplinary colleagues' expertise in a myriad of ways through afterschool, before-school, or lunchtime co-sponsorships.

Then there are intra- and extra-district partnerships with entities that offer existing afterschool programs, such as the language-support services department collaboration noted earlier, public libraries, and institutions of higher learning.

Strong school districts understand the value of strong collaborative partnerships with stakeholders. District stakeholders include students, teachers, school and district administrators, and community members. Teachers who work in schools without an operational policy to handle parental challenges should work with the school district stakeholders to develop an operation policy. The policy should include easily accessible procedures and clear timelines that will indicate when challenges would be addressed.

As mentioned previously, the formation of local and regional collaboratives will continue to build momentum and gain support for maintaining classrooms that are rich with opportunities for students to build their foundational skills and go on to become the next generation of society builders.

References

Anderson, M. T. (2002). *Feed.* Candlewick Press.

Brnovich, M., Cameron, D., Carr, C. M., Fitch, L., Hunter, M., Knudsen, A., Landry, J., Marshall, S., Morrisey, P., Paxton, K., Peterson, D., Reyes, S., Rokita, T., Rutledge, L., Schmidt, D., Schmitt, E., Taylor, T., Wasden, L., Wilson, A., & Yost, D. (2021, May 19). *Re: Comments on proposed priorities—American history and civics education docket ID ED-2021OESE-0033.* https://content.govdelivery.com/attachments/INAG/2021/05/19/file_attachments/1812972/DOE%20Letter.pdf

Chbosky, S. (1999). *The perks of being a wallflower.* Pocket Books.

Creswell, J. W., & Creswell, J. D. (2023). *Research design: Qualitative, quantitative, and mixed methods approaches* (6th ed.). SAGE.

Feingold, J., & Weishart, J. (2023). *How discriminatory censorship laws imperil public education.* National Education Policy Center.

Healy-Cullen, S., Taylor, J. E., Ross, K., & Morison, T. (2022). Youth encounters with internet pornography: A survey of youth, caregiver, and educator perspectives. *Sexuality & Culture, 26*(2), 491–513. https://doi.org/10.1007/s12119-021-09904-y

Hosseini, K. (2018). *The kite runner.* Bloomsbury.

Jarreau, A. (2012). Intuiting the unknown: Listening with the unconscious mind. *Modern Psychoanalysis, 37*(1), 66–81.

Kobabe, M. (2019). *Gender queer: A memoir.* Lion Forge.

Maxwell, J. A. (2013). *Qualitative research design: An interactive approach* (3rd ed.). SAGE.

Meehan, K., Baêta, S., Markham, M., & Magnusson, T. (2024, April 16). *Banned in the USA: Narrating the crisis.* PEN America. https://pen.org/report/narrating-the-crisis/

Mental Health America. (2023). *Looking back: The history of Mental Health America.* https://mhanational.org/our-history

Merriam, S., & Tisdell, E. (2016). *Qualitative research: A guide to design and implementation* (4th ed.). Jossey-Bass.

Miles, M. B., Huberman, A. M., & Saldana, J. (2014). *Qualitative data analysis: A methods sourcebook* (3rd ed.). SAGE.

Pulitzer Center Education. (2022). *Applications open: The 1619 Project Afterschool Partnership program.* https://1619education.org/id/node/27870

Pulitzer Center Education. (2022). *Erasure poetry as resistance.* https://app.mizzenapp.org/curricula/ckpxaom2w37a007331dkmsvh8

Pulitzer Center Education. (2022). *Introducing The 1619 project.* https://app.mizzenapp.org/curricula/ckpg1kylj29f80733fs2de4st

Rodriguez, J. A. (2017). *House built on ashes: A memoir.* University of Oklahoma Press.

U.S. Geological Survey. (2021). *Texas and Landsat.* https://www.usgs.gov/publications/texas-and-landsat

S.B. 3, 87th Leg., 2nd Sess.(Tex. 2021). https://capitol.texas.gov/tlodocs/872/billtext/pdf/SB00003I.pdf

"Lots of Ways to Be Brave": A Teacher's Guide to Facing Censorship

CHRISTINA L. DOBBS
ANNAMARY CONSALVO
KATHARINE COVINO
ANN D. DAVID
CHRISTINE EMERAN
PAMELA A. MASON

Members of NCTE's Standing Committee Against Censorship offer an overview of the landscape of censorship; the ways teachers can prepare, respond, and report censorship; and NCTE resources that support teachers.

Seems to me there are lots of ways to be brave.
—Katherine Applegate, an author whose book *Wishtree* was recently challenged In Florida

These days, materials used in American classrooms are increasingly seen as not neutral. Every book, story, and resource can come under scrutiny by an increasingly wide range of people outside a school or library, and it takes many acts of bravery, small and large, to start or continue teaching about certain stories. When it comes to censorship challenges, it's not a question of *if*, but *when*. Even long-accepted and beloved books can find themselves on the banned list. Every book or text seems to be open for debate and, possibly, for removal.

Censorship in the United States is increasing in a number of concerning ways that are important for teachers to both understand and prepare to face. Book bans are increasing across the country, driven by a range of different forces and parties (Alter). A recent report by PEN America indicated an increase of 28 percent in book bans in fall 2022 as compared with the first half the year; they recorded 1,477 cases of banning individual books, including 874 unique titles, with a special focus on stories featuring people of color or LGBTQ+ people (Meehan and Friedman).

But these statistics do not capture the full extent of efforts to censor books, which are increasingly orchestrated by organizations who seek to ban large swaths of books or to support legislation seeking to impose wide-spanning limits on reading material in schools

Reprinted from *English Journal*,*113*(3), 2024, pp. 22–28
DOI: https://doi.org/10.58680/ej2024113322

(Alter). The legislative path to censorship is widening—as of February 14, 2023, eighty-six gag orders limiting educational materials have been introduced in a range of states (Friedman et al.), a practice which seems to be continuing (Meehan and Friedman). These policies, which can even dictate how teachers add new titles to their classroom collections, are important to understand, as they may impact many facets of curriculum or independent reading planning at a school.

But these stances represent the agenda of a relative few. A recent survey from the American Library Association (ALA) revealed that most voters do not support book banning efforts affecting local libraries, including majorities of Democrats, Republicans, and independent voters ("Large Majorities of Voters"). This survey also showed a majority of voters' confidence in libraries, and it affirmed that various types of books that have been banned should be available in school libraries. While less is known about support for teaching particular materials, this widespread support is an important, if quiet, part of the story of increased censorship in the United States.

And in an age of rising censorship, it is more important than ever for teachers and other school personnel to take steps to prepare themselves for challenges to books, curricula, and other pedagogical activities (like discussion or essay prompts) before those challenges occur. But our work as members of NCTE's Standing Committee Against Censorship and our work with the National Coalition Against Censorship (NCAC) have shown us that many teachers and schools are not sure how to prepare for censorship challenges or how to act when challenges occur. Here, we hope to support practitioners in building brave systems for facing censorship, so we present our best collaborative advice to be as prepared as possible for censorship challenges, including what to do before, during, and after to advocate for intellectual freedom and the freedom to read in your own school community.

Prepare: Before a Challenge

One key step to being ready for a challenge is thoughtful and multifaceted preparation before one even takes place. First, before discussing any particular texts or instructional choices, consider your own context and take several proactive steps. Knowing the policy implications and history of challenges in your school or district is an important element of being prepared. Some simple steps might help with this sort of preparation:

- Ask administrators about existing policies regarding censorship. Sometimes policies exist and are current and ready for implementation. Other times, old policies are on the books that have long ceased to be enforced, or there may be outdated policies that will be enacted should a challenge arise. Knowing about these ahead of time can help you navigate a challenge if one occurs.
- If no such censorship policies exist or your school needs to update its policies, encourage your administrators to build a multiparty plan and policy to face challenges. By assembling an array of interested parties, including teachers, administrators, students, and caregivers (the variety of adults who might support students as they progress through school), a collaborative and thoughtful approach to discussing challenges can be built. Having a plan in place that in-

cludes input from various parties will aid in following policies when challenges occur.

- Do some research about the history of challenges in your area. This might include talking with librarians, looking into local media archives, or seeking stories from those who have been in the community a long while. This research may help you understand your context more fully and see what issues have been at the heart of prior challenges.
- Identify and connect with local advocates for intellectual freedom to see what resources are available to you and get advice for advocating for free speech in your community. These might include organizations that advocate for free speech or defend against censorship, including your local chapter of NCTE.

Gaining a thorough understanding of the challenge process, if it exists, will allow teachers, curriculum specialists, department leaders, and administrators to be conversant in it and proactive in using it. Having a brave system in place prior to a challenge means that individuals do not need to decide what to do in a moment of crisis (Clear).

> Inviting adult caregivers to read alongside your students or sharing a process for communicating concerns can go a long way toward building honest and open communication and possibly staving off a broad challenge.

Early in the school year, there are additional steps you can take that are specific to your classroom. You might send a communication to your students and their adult caregivers to share some broad strokes of your curriculum and goals, your expectations for independent reading, or how to monitor and participate in their students' reading choices or your classroom instructional choices. Inviting adult caregivers to read alongside your students or sharing a process for communicating concerns can go a long way toward building honest and open communication and possibly staving off a broad challenge. This could involve general written communications in languages that community members use, interactive conversations at school open-house events, invitations to community members to visit the classroom, or communication with caregivers immediately prior to engaging with potentially controversial materials.

We also invite you to consider the possibility of challenges early. This is not to say you should self-censor or decide not to teach something because you fear a challenge; rather, you can critically evaluate the possibilities for challenges to a given text. A key first step is introspection and reflection. As part of the book (or other text) selection process—long before a challenge occurs—teachers should carefully consider their reasons for selecting a book or resource. Perhaps it aligns with and supports specific curriculum standards. Or maybe it represents a key issue, voice, or experience that needs exploration.

A helpful guide for teachers interested in asking these types of questions is NCTE's This Story Matters project website (see Important Links sidebar). The site offers educators rationales for frequently challenged books. For teachers who are selecting books, reading rationales is likely to foreground and support reflection on important issues regarding text selection. Part of the process may include a consideration of other titles that meet the curriculum standards that could be offered to caregivers as alternatives. Planning alternative texts is not defeatist; it is just good sense and good practice—similar to planning for differentiation.

Before you decide to use a book in your instruction, you can also read reviews of the book from various sources that are known for providing clear information, including recommendations for age ranges for various titles. Reviews will likely address topics that are the target of book challenges right now, especially LGBTQ+ characters and storylines that take on racism and privilege. As you think about these possible objections, you should consider your school context and ask yourself a few questions:

- How would you address objections from your constituents (learners, colleagues, administration, families, community members) were they to raise concerns about this title?
- Are there marginalized groups that would feel that the text selection did not appropriately represent their culture, language, and ways of being, knowing, and doing? How might you address these feelings about representation and teach students to read critically with regard to how groups are represented?
- Are there content standards that you think this title will address fully? Are there alternatives?
- Can you connect this text to broader curricular goals or essential questions, the school's literacy goals for student outcomes, or the school's mission, strategic plan, or commitments to inclusion and equity?
- Could you plan to provide information about possible objections people might have to a particular text? Could you prepare to support community members in discussing the text in a way that invites them to participate in community discussion?

At this early stage, it would be helpful to confer with your colleagues. You may find the resources provided by the National Council of Teachers of English and the National Coalition Against Censorship informative as you define your teaching and learning goals and as you anticipate possible objections to the texts you have selected.

Some teachers, though, work at sites where they may not have the support of the administration in teaching topics deemed controversial. It is key to understand whether your leaders and colleagues are supportive of your choice to use a particular text. So you might ask around to get a feel for whether this support exists, find out whether other teachers also want to teach the text, and understand the general feeling toward the choice going into the school's teaching. And of course, you might also have an alternative book selection ready to go, in case a challenge comes to you.

An important ally in selecting and teaching diverse books is the school librarian, who has a wealth of knowledge about the community, the school administration, and the literature available.

Allies can also be found outside the school. Community librarians are often strong allies and can play a role in bolstering community support for text inclusion. Caregivers, community members, and school stakeholders are more likely to support teaching decisions when they feel their voices have been heard and respected. These preparation steps can help schools and districts have productive conversations about potential censorship, help community members feel they have means to participate in conversations about censorship, and aid individual teachers in effectively planning for instruction in a climate of censorship. But unfortunately, doing this work does not mean a challenge will not occur.

Respond and Report: During a Challenge

It sometimes starts with an email, phone call, or visit from an administrator: "Someone's complained." Many book challenges today, though, do not start with a parent calling or emailing you and objecting to their child reading an assigned book. They start when a parent or community member goes to the principal, superintendent, or school board with a list of ten or twenty books and asks that those books be reconsidered or banned. You, a teacher who picked one of these books, might find out after some part of this challenge process has begun, or as the process unfolds before your eyes and books are pulled off library and classroom shelves.

You will almost certainly have strong feelings in this moment, and you are not alone in those feelings, which might include shame, disappointment, and anger. These are real and visceral and felt by all teachers who are faced with book challenges. Taking care of yourself in the midst of these powerful feelings is a key step in responding to a challenge. Here are some tips:

- Include at least one colleague in the conversation with your administrator to help you remember details later.
- Take notes while you are talking, because feelings get in the way of memory. Try to get as much information as possible about the situation.
- Remind the administrator, if necessary, of the existing policy for book challenges (if there is one, and hopefully there is) and, if possible, have a link saved on your computer to the policy or have a printed copy to hand them.
- Ask which specific "next steps" are your responsibility, to ensure that whatever the process is, you know your role.
- Follow up on the conversation with an email, or reply to the initial email, summarizing the conversation and the expectations for your actions, as a way to create an internal paper trail.

It is also important that you know your rights in this challenge process, something you have hopefully researched already. But if not, it is essential to find out a few answers. Do you get to keep teaching the book? Can copies of the book stay available to students? Are you responsible for turning over curricular documents? At every point in this process, remind everyone involved to return to the process's steps and expectations. That brave system can help you keep the book in your classroom and in students' hands.

> You will almost certainly have strong feelings, which might include shame, disappointment, and anger. Taking care of yourself in the midst of these powerful feelings is a key step in responding to a challenge.

Following your initial response to the challenge to your materials, it is also essential to report the situation. A number of organizations track book challenges (e.g., NCAC, ALA) for information purposes as well as to aid educators with resources and support. It is easy to report a challenge:

- If you are an NCTE member, you can go to NCTE's Intellectual Freedom Center website and from there, click on "Report

Censorship" to navigate to the incident report form. The form will ask about the nature of what happened and the context in which it occurred. Teachers' names are kept confidential even as the incident is investigated.

- Once an incident is reported, NCTE coordinates with its partners at NCAC, PEN America, and ALA on letters of support, materials for teachers, and various other kinds of direct support.
- Censorship incidents can also be reported through NCAC's website. NCAC has a broader focus on censorship, and collects incidents from schools, libraries, museums, and any other venue or organization. Like NCTE, NCAC keeps reporters' names confidential. The NCAC form can also be shared with caregivers and community members to report censorship happening in local schools. The response time is not long: reporters usually hear back in one to three days.

Important Links

NCTE's This Story Matters rationale database: https://ncte.org/book-rationales/this-story-matters/

NCTE censorship incident report form: ncte.org/report-censorship-incident/

NCAC censorship incident report form: ncac.org/report-censorship

Considerations and guidelines for school officials: ncac.org/news/blog/guidelines-school-officials

NCAC School Book Challenge Resource Center: ncac.org/resource/book-challenge-resource-center

Sample school board policy for adopting new instructional materials (from Hamilton Southeastern Schools):

go.boarddocs.com/in/hses/Board.nsf /goto?open &id=86X5PB6D719F

Repair and Reflect: After a Challenge

After a challenge occurs, it can be difficult to determine next steps, and the process may vary depending on whether a challenge was successful or not. While far less has been written about what follows a book challenge in a community, it is important to consider what to do after, in order to reflect on the processes and policies a school has regarding censorship, as well as to repair communities that may have been damaged as a result of book challenges.

First, if a challenge did not succeed in removing a book from your classroom but some students will not have access to it, it may be key to consider how those students might continue learning and participating in your classroom community. It can be isolating to be the only one or one of a few reading a particular text, while everyone else in class is reading a text together. It can be important to find ways to include students in the work of the class community even as they may be pursuing an alternative curriculum. Often it is not students themselves who choose not to read a particular text, so ensuring they feel included will be essential to the broader health of your classroom community.

Additionally, you might consider how and why you might continue discussing the challenge, whether it was successful or not:

First consider discussions that might be had with the school's staff and faculty:

- Does it make sense to appeal the decision if it resulted in a book or other text being banned?
- Do interested parties need more discussion about their rights?
- Are there elements of the current policy that might be improved or refined based on what happened?
- Do we need to seek advice from the union, anti-censorship organizations, or legal entities to clarify or help us move forward?
- Do we need more discussion or preparation in how to present controversial material in ways that are less likely to result in challenges?
- How can we continue to include the families of students who supported a book challenge in our community?
- Can we facilitate additional conversations (that might include the community) about curriculum or books more broadly to look ahead to instruction in future semesters or years?
- Are teachers and staff handling the stress and conflict of a book challenge effectively and with their own well-being in mind? Do they need mental health supports or other structural supports as they reflect on this process?

Then consider potentially valuable conversations about/with students who may or may not be aware that a challenge has taken place:

- Do students want to have more information about censorship and their own rights as readers (or writers)?
- How can the school community support students who feel marginalized by the challenge?
- Do we need to do some community-building work to ensure that all students (including those whose stories were challenged) feel like valued and validated members of our classroom communities?
- Do we need mental health or counseling supports for students who might have felt their identities were attacked or marginalized in the process of a book challenge?

It is likely that following a book challenge process, those most heavily involved might feel exhausted or upset, depending on how things were decided. We do not suggest that teachers undertake all of these steps immediately or even ever, depending on how they might be feeling. Our fear in moving forward without discussing an event that can be traumatizing for community members is that the sense of stress and unease will only continue, and an opportunity will be missed to move ahead in a way that supports all involved.

A Closing Note on Using This Guide

We know how disheartening it can be to feel as though even the most traditional of texts, such as *To Kill a Mockingbird*, are under fire in this age of censorship. We know how stressful it can be to spend time and energy working to build an effective, critical, and equity-minded curriculum, only to have it challenged. We deeply admire the teachers and schools who insist on ensuring that students have the freedom to read, have the right to see their own stories in books, and have the right to learn history from the perspectives of all who were involved.

And so, it is our sincerest hope that you will find actionable ideas in this *before, during,* and *after* guide to help you face the challenges that seem inevitable. We hope that you will find strategies, resources, and ideas for moving your own community forward in advocating for intellectual freedom. The NCTE position statement on *The Students' Right to Read* states, "One of the foundations of a democratic society is the individual's right to read, and also the individual's right to freely choose what they would like to read." We know that now, more than ever, it can seem challenging to ensure students' freedom to read. But you are not alone in this work, and we are grateful for all who work toward standing up to censorship in all its forms, in all the many ways of being brave. Doing so is nothing short of working to safeguard a key foundation of our democratic society.

Works Cited

Alter, Alexandra. "Book Bans Rising Rapidly in the US, Free Speech Groups Find." *The New York Times*, 20 Apr. 2023, www.nytimes.com/2023/04/20/books/book-bans-united-states-free-speech.html.

Clear, James. *Atomic Habits: An Easy and Proven Way to Build Good Habits and Break Bad Ones.* Avery Books, 2018.

Friedman, Jonathan, et al. "Educational Censorship Continues: The 2023 Legislative Sessions So Far." *PEN America,* 16 Feb. 2023, pen.org/educational-censorship-continues-in-2023/.

"Large Majorities of Voters Oppose Book Bans and Have Confidence in Libraries." *American Library Association*, 24 Mar. 2022, www.ala.org/news/press-releases/2022/03 /large-majorities-voters-oppose-book-bans-and-have-confidence-libraries. Press release.

Meehan, Kasey, and Jonathan Friedman. "Banned in the USA: State Laws Supercharge Book Suppression in Schools." *PEN America,* 20 Apr. 2023, pen.org/report/banned-in-the-usa-state-laws-supercharge-book-suppression-in-schools/.

The Students' Right to Read. National Council of Teachers of English, 25 Oct. 2018, ncte.org/statement/righttoread guideline/. Position statement.

INDEX

ABOUT THE CONTRIBUTORS

Annamary Consalvo, professor of literacy at The University of Texas at Tyler and past chair of NCTE's Committee Against Censorship, taught courses in teacher preparation and research methods. A former English teacher, her research interests included the teaching of writing, ways in which preservice teachers' learning is best supported, and ways in which young adult literature can be used to open essential conversations.

Katharine Covino, associate professor of English studies, teaches writing, literature, and teacher-preparation classes at Fitchburg State University. Her current scholarship explores critical pedagogy, applying indigenous lenses to cultural myths, and action research with English teachers. Covino has recently been published in *Teaching/Writing: The Journal of Writing Teacher Education*, *English Journal*, and has contributed chapters to a number of edited collections. She recently served as a coeditor on two different volumes focused on critical pedagogy: *Challenging Bias and Promoting Transformative Education in Public Schooling Through Critical Literacy* and *The Intersections of Critical Pedagogy, Critical Literacy, and Social Justice: Empowerment, Equity, and Education for Liberation*. The latter recently won a 2024 AESA Critics Choice Award. Prior to university teaching, she taught middle school and high school English in Austin, Texas.

Susan Cridland-Hughes is an associate professor in the College of Education at Clemson University, where she teaches courses in cultural diversity and middle and secondary English methods. Her research focuses on the intersections of social justice, critical literacy, and orality in out-of-school educational spaces, looking particularly at debate pedagogy and debate education. Her most recent research project investigates the nationwide expansion of book bans and the policies governing book challenges in public schools. Her work has been featured in the *Journal of Language and Literacy Education*, *Journal of Adolescent Literacy*, and *English Teaching: Practice and Critique*.

Jed Cridland-Hughes is the Public Services Librarian at Spartanburg Community College in Spartanburg, South Carolina, where he coordinates and provides library instruction for the college. Before entering the library field, he taught high school English in the Baltimore City Public Schools for six years. After earning a master's degree in library and information science from Florida State University, he has worked in public and private law libraries, a public library system, and now an academic library. His most recent research explores book bans in public and school libraries.

Ann D. David is the chair of NCTE's Committee Against Censorship and a professor at the University of the Incarnate Word. Her current scholarship explores the teaching of writing in complex and complicated secondary contexts. Her edited collection *When Teaching Writing Gets Tough: Challenges and Possibilities in Secondary Writing Instruction* was published by Teachers College Press. Additionally, her research explores the textual milieu of censorship, including its impacts on English teachers, by using arts-based methods. Serving as the librettist alongside composer Dr. Kevin Salfen, *Five Choral Risks* will premiere in 2025. Her advocacy for teachers' right to teach and students' right to read has led to opportunities to present on censorship and its impacts at the state and national level.

Christina L. Dobbs is an associate professor and program director of English Education for Equity and Justice at the Wheelock College of Education and Human Development at Boston University. Her research focuses on disciplinary literacy, language diversity, teacher beliefs and professional learning, and organizational change. Her forthcoming books are titled *Until Every Woman Is Free: A Duoethnographic Exploration of Equity and Belonging in the Academy* and *Critical Disciplinary Literacy: An Equity-Driven and Culturally Responsive Approach to Disciplinary Teaching and Learning.* She grew up in rural Texas and is a former English/language arts teacher and reading specialist.

Christine Emeran is director of the Youth Free Expression Program at the National Coalition Against Censorship. She writes on contemporary issues about young people, social media, and social movements in the United States and Europe. Emeran is a Fulbright fellow and author of *New Generation Political Activism in Ukraine 2000–2014*, a book chapter on generational change and the personalization of protest included in a global social movement book series, *When Students Protest: Secondary and High Schools,* a book chapter on school censorship and student protest in a book manuscript, *Sociological Research and Urban Children and Youth,* and a book chapter on book censorship to be featured in *Project Censored's State of the Free Press.* She has taught at Manhattan College and St. John's University in New York and at Sciences Po in Paris, France, and received a PhD in sociology from the New School for Social Research.

Jennifer Gallman is a high school English teacher of seventeen years in South Carolina and a doctoral candidate in the Department of Teaching and Learning at Clemson University. Her research focuses on social justice curriculum and censorship in public high schools. Other research interests include fighting against educational gag orders in the United States.

Ricki Ginsberg is an associate professor of English education at Colorado State University. Her research focuses on supporting teachers with censorship and intellectual freedom, reimagining literacy practices to be grounded in local communities, and recruiting and retaining teachers of color. She is a former ALAN president and a former editor of *The ALAN Review*. Her work has been published in journals including *American Indian Quarterly, English Journal, Reading Research Quarterly, Research in the Teaching of English,* and *Teachers College Record.* Her most recent published book is titled *Challenging Traditional Classroom Spaces with YA Literature: Students in Community as Course Co-Designers* (2022, NCTE).

Melanie D. Koss is a professor of literacy education in the Department of Curriculum and Instruction at Northern Illinois University. Her research interests include examining representations of diversity in children's and young adult literature and literature awards, advocating against antisemitism and for Jewish inclusion through children's and young adult literature, the role of teacher autonomy in the selection of children's and young adult literature for the curriculum and in classroom libraries, and the implications of censorship and book banning in the classroom.

Mark Letcher is an associate professor of English education and director of the English Language Arts Teaching program at Lewis University in Romeoville, Illinois. His research and teaching specialize in preservice teacher education, writing teacher education, and adolescent literature and literacies. He also has served since 2021 as the Executive Director of the Assembly on Literature for Adolescents of NCTE (ALAN). His work has been published in journals such as *English Journal, The ALAN Review, English Education, Research in the Teaching of English, College Composition and Communication, Teaching/Writing: The Journal of Writing Teacher Education,* and *Voices from the Middle.* He has also published work on young adult literature in a number of edited collections.

Pamela A. Mason is a senior lecturer on education and director of the Jeanne Chall Reading Lab at the Harvard Graduate School of Education. Mason collaborates with colleagues nationally and globally on preparing reading specialist teachers and literacy coaches and evaluating schoolwide literacy programs.

Alisia N. Muir is a National Board-certified teacher who lives and teaches in El Paso, Texas. She conducts research on the perceptions of dual residents in the US border region. Her work focuses on building a beloved community, nonviolence, justice, and peace studies.

James O'Keeffe taught secondary and postsecondary English language arts in Texas schools and colleges for twenty-five years. He is a graduate of the University of Texas at El Paso with an MFA in creative writing, and he now spends his time on advocacy and freelance writing.

Kathleen A. Paciga is a professor emerita of education at Columbia College Chicago. Her work examines early literacy development, early childhood literacy instruction and assessment, and the integration of children's literature and media into children's literate lives.

This book was typeset in PT Sans, PT Sans Narrow, and Alternate Gothic No3 by Barbara Frazier.

The typefaces used on the cover include Avenir Next Condensed Demi Bold, Impact, Akzidenz Grotesk Std., Akzidenz Grotesk BQ, and Source Sans Pro.

The book was printed on 50 lb., white offset paper.